America in the Progressive Era, 1890–1914

We work with leading authors to develop the
strongest educational materials in history,
bringing cutting-edge thinking and best learning
practice to a global market.

Under a range of well-known imprints, including
Longman, we craft high-quality print and electronic
publications which help readers to understand and
apply their content, whether studying or at work.

To find out more about the complete range of our
publishing please visit us on the World Wide Web at:
www.pearsoneduc.com

SEMINAR STUDIES IN HISTORY

America in the Progressive Era, 1890–1914

LEWIS L. GOULD

An imprint of Pearson Education

Harlow, England · London · New York · Reading, Massachusetts · San Francisco · Toronto · Don Mills, Ontario · Sydney
Tokyo · Singapore · Hong Kong · Seoul · Taipei · Cape Town · Madrid · Mexico City · Amsterdam · Munich · Paris · Milan

Pearson Education Limited
Edinburgh Gate
Harlow
Essex CM20 2JE
England
and Associated Companies throughout the world.

Visit us on the World Wide Web at:
www.pearsoneduc.com

First published 2001

© Pearson Education Limited 2001

ISBN 0-582-35671-7 PPR

British Library Cataloguing-in-Publication Data
A catalogue record for this book is
available from the British Library

Library of Congress Cataloging-in-Publication Data
Gould, Lewis L.
    The progressive era: America, 1890-1914 / Lewis L. Gould.
        p. cm. -- (Seminar studies in history)
    Includes bibliographical references and index.
    ISBN 0-582-35671-7 (pbk.)
        1. United States--Politics and government--1865-1933. 2. Progressivism (United States
    politics) 3. United States--Social conditions--1865-1918. 4. United States--Economic
    conditions--1865-1918. I. Series.

E661 .G675 2000
973.91--dc21   00-042117

Set by 7 in 10/12 Sabon Roman
Printed in Malaysia ,LSP

CONTENTS

INTRODUCTION TO THE SERIES

Such is the pace of historical enquiry in the modern world that there is an ever-widening gap between the specialist article or monograph, incorporating the results of current research, and general surveys, which inevitably become out of date. Seminar Studies in History are designed to bridge this gap. The series was founded by Patrick Richardson in 1966 and his aim was to cover major themes in British, European and world history. Between 1980 and 1996 Roger Lockyer continued his work, before handing the editorship over to Clive Emsley and Gordon Martel. Clive Emsley is Professor of History at the Open University, while Gordon Martel is Professor of International History at the University of Northern British Columbia, Canada, and Senior Research Fellow at De Montfort University.

All the books are written by experts in their field who are not only familiar with the latest research but have often contributed to it. They are frequently revised, in order to take account of new information and interpretations. They provide a selection of documents to illustrate major themes and provoke discussion, and also a guide to further reading. The aim of Seminar Studies is to clarify complex issues without over-simplifying them, and to stimulate readers into deepening their knowledge and understanding of major themes and topics.

NOTE ON REFERENCING SYSTEM

Readers should note that numbers in square brackets [5] refer them to the corresponding entry in the Bibliography at the end of the book (specific page numbers are given in italics). A number in square brackets preceded by *Doc.* [*Doc. 5*] refers readers to the corresponding item in the Documents section which follows the main text.

During the quarter of a century that elapsed between 1890 and 1914, the United States went through a period of political, social, and economic reform that has come to be known as the 'Progressive Era.' By the time that World War I erupted in Europe during the summer of 1914, the public life of the United States had undergone significant changes that shaped the domestic agenda of the nation for the rest of the twentieth century. Because the Progressive Era was so central to the way the history of the United States unfolded for the next eight decades, scholars have devoted extensive attention and voluminous writing to understanding what happened and why [110].

By 1914, the national government had adopted policies to intervene in the workings of the economy and to regulate the behavior of individuals and corporations in society that would have seemed inconceivable to the politicians and the public twenty-five years earlier. By the second year of Woodrow Wilson's presidency, the United States had created a central banking mechanism (the Federal Reserve system), adopted an income tax, established national regulatory agencies (the Federal Trade Commission), and amended the Constitution to have senators elected by the people rather than by state legislatures. Vigorous campaigns to grant the vote to women and to prohibit the sale and manufacture of alcoholic beverages were under way. As one progressive from Texas put it in 1910, more and more Americans now believed that governments were created 'for the protection of the weak against the encroachments of the strong' and served as 'the familiar forum of the contest between the strong and the weak, the powerful and the helpless, the many and the few, between the general and the special interests' [53 p. 26].

Twenty-five years earlier, the agenda of the national government had been very different. In the Fifty-First Congress that met during 1889–90, there were some stirrings of protest against big business that expressed themselves in the passage of the Sherman Antitrust Act (1890), but the major issues involved such perennial questions as the nature of the currency, the use of tariffs to protect American industry from foreign competition, and the honesty and fairness of elections in the South where African Americans faced racial discrimination. Where the public men and women of 1914 were debating how much government should intervene in the economy, their counterparts in 1890 were still engaged in the discussion that had shaped American politics for much of the nineteenth century: what was the best means by which government at all levels could promote the growth and expansion of the economy? The shift from government as an instrument of promotion to a means of regulation was one of the key developments of the progressive spirit [28; 48].

A second change between 1890 and 1914 had to do with the role and place of the political party in making decisions about the future of the nation. In 1890 the two major political parties, the Republicans and the Democrats, were in charge of how candidates were selected, elections were held, and policies were adopted. Male citizens were intensely partisan and were convinced that political parties were the best means to conduct public life. American white men, the holders of the right to vote in most of the country, turned out for elections at rates that would not be matched in the next century. In the northern and middle western states, turnouts of 70–80 percent in presidential elections were commonplace. As one politician put it, 'We love our parties as we love our churches and our families. We are part of them' [20 *p. 215*]. Allegiance to a party was one of the ways that Americans defined their place in the community.

By 1914, devotion to parties had receded. Independent voters had become a major element in national elections, and suspicion of partisanship had become commonplace. Such innovations as the 'direct primary' to choose candidates for elections, the 'initiative' to propose legislation, the 'recall' to oust unpopular officials, and the 'referendum' to put specific issues before the voters, had all sapped the power of the parties to set the political agenda. In addition to these procedural changes, the emergence of the regulatory agencies to set public policy had shifted authority and influence away from the politicians. In elections themselves, fewer voters turned out even as participation in contests became easier. One of the notable features of the progressive spirit was the actual decline it produced in the involvement of Americans in their government and public life. That development proved to be one of the important unintended consequences of an age of reform [35; 104].

The way in which Americans governed themselves in their cities and states also underwent significant changes during these twenty-five years. In municipal government, the Progressive Era saw a shift from a reliance on strong mayors and geographically based city councils to newer concepts such as rule by commissioners linked to specific responsibilities such as fire and police or even a city-manager. The larger thrust was toward removing politics from how cities were run and relying more on non-partisanship [107].

In the states, the political parties were in the ascendancy in 1890 amid popular complaints of 'rings' and 'machines' in the statehouses and legisla-

tures. By 1914 reform governors had appeared in many states, and regulatory agencies had been established to conduct many of the expanded
functions of the state government. The result was governments that were
freer of corruption and more efficient. They were also in some instances less
responsive to the voters as a whole [26 *pp. 230–2*].

Historians have differed strongly ever since the end of the Progressive
Era about its meaning and significance. In the 1950s, Richard Hofstadter
advanced what became known as the 'status' interpretation when he argued
that a perceived loss of social and economic status animated the reformers
[31]. A few years later in the early 1960s, Gabriel Kolko contended that
business interests used the rhetoric of reform to stave off more sweeping
political and economic change. Accordingly, the era saw what he called the
'Triumph of Conservatism' [32].

A decade later, David Thelen returned to the interpretations set out at
the time to argue that unhappy consumers and individual citizens, aroused
by the inequities revealed during the Depression of the 1890s, banded
together to seek social change [59]. Robert M. Crunden in the early 1980s
stressed the religious backgrounds of 'Ministers of Reform' as a key element
in their decision to pursue reform in the public sector [25]. During the
1990s scholars have shifted attention away from politics as a central
element in progressivism and explored in more detail the social dimensions
of reform. Greater attention has been devoted to the role of women in
providing support and leadership for progressive change [26].

Through all of these professional arguments about the exact character of
reform in the early twentieth century, historians have disagreed about
whether it represented an authentic political reform movement that addressed real injustices or an elitist campaign to prevent more sweeping
changes in the nation. Was progressivism a precursor to the New Deal of
Franklin D. Roosevelt and the Great Society of Lyndon Johnson, or was it
something special only in its own time and circumstances? Even such
seemingly direct and straightforward questions as 'who were the progressives?' have resulted in complex and contradictory answers about the
membership of the movement. Definitions of progressivism became so loose
and ill-defined that one historian a generation ago suggested that the term
'progressive movement' had lost all of its substantive meaning [106].

Yet for all of its contradictions and ambiguities, the Progressive Era was
something real in the history of the United States. The ways in which
Americans ran their government and ordered their lives were very different
in 1914 from how they had been in 1890. Social and technological changes
accounted for some of these transformations, but there had also been a
significant shift in the attitudes toward what government should do and
how its affairs should be conducted. In the process, the United States
became a more just and equitable nation than it had been in 1890. Not all

ills had been cured, but significant advances had taken place. Most important, the Progressive Era had defined the agenda of American domestic
reform for much of the twentieth century that followed.

This book traces the origins and growth of reform in the 1890s, looks at
the role of the presidencies of Theodore Roosevelt and Woodrow Wilson in
bringing progressivism to the national stage, and attempts to provide an
analytic narrative that relates intellectual trends, local events, and national
currents for the years from 1890 to 1914. While the American progressives
deserve criticism for their shortcomings, they also should receive credit for
the positive changes they made in the life of their country.

AUTHOR'S ACKNOWLEDGEMENTS

This book owes much to the experience of teaching undergraduate and graduate courses in the Gilded Age and Progressive Era to students at the University of Texas at Austin between 1967 and 1998. The students provided close attention and stimulating ideas. I am grateful to Gordon Martel for asking me to undertake this project. Karen Gould gave generous support and timely inspiration at key moments to make the book possible.

Austin Texas
February 2000

PUBLISHER'S ACKNOWLEDGEMENTS

We are grateful to the following for permission to reproduce copyright material:

State Historical Society of Iowa for extracts from a letter from Charles E. Perkins to Senator William Boyd Allison 26.2.1906 and the Jonathan Dolliver papers, letter of James S. Clarkson to Dolliver 6.3.1906 and The Center for American History for an extract from the Terrell speech to the National Civic Federation, New York City 1906, Terrell Papers Box 2H17; Punch Limited for the two cartoons 'The Rough Rider' and 'Platform Amenities'; photograph of Woodrow Wilson reproduced courtesy of Popperfoto; Chicago Historical Society for the reproduction of a portrait of Jane Addams, Chicago (Ill) 1893, creator Alice Kellogg Tyler.

PART ONE   BACKGROUND

CHAPTER ONE

THE ROOTS OF PROGRESSIVE CHANGE

The origins of the Progressive Era can be extended back into the 1880s, but the outlines of what would become the reform campaign began to appear about 1890. In a number of areas, Americans identified major social problems, called for an expanded role for the state, and pursued a more active regulatory government. The older beliefs in a government that encouraged enterprise, but did not regulate it, yielded slowly to these newer attitudes.

Twenty-five years after the end of the Civil War in 1865, the United States had become a major economic power. There were 63 million Americans in 1895, most of whom still lived in rural areas. The growth of cities had marked the years since the South had surrendered. More than 22 million people lived in towns and cities of more than 2,500 residents by 1890, and the increasing perception of urban problems would be a major force in the progressive reform spirit. The nation had also become industrialized, with 250,000 miles of railroad track, the most in the world. Of the nation's gross national product of $27 billion (expressed in 1929 dollars), non-farm products contributed some $20 billion of the total. With the rise of manufacturing, issues of regulating the burgeoning industries were coming to the fore.

The railroads, for example, were the first big business. The lines employed thousands of people and did business in many different states. The rates that they set affected whether countless shippers made or lost money in carrying on a business. The ability of the rail lines to determine the economic health of a town or city, their direct impact on the lives of farmers and manufacturers, and their capacity to influence legislatures and courts all made the railroads a significant political issue. By 1890 the United States had already begun to oversee the operations of rail lines through state regulatory commissions and the Interstate Commerce Commission (created in 1887). For many Americans, the interstate railroads remained an economic power that seemed outside the bounds of government control.

One reason that government seemed such an unlikely opponent for concentrated economic power in the last decade of the nineteenth century was its relatively small size compared to the reach of the national government a century later. The government in Washington affected the average citizen of the United States only in small ways in 1890. The main body of employees of the federal government worked in the Post Office Department or in the armed services. The army and navy were small forces, and the primary task of the 25,000-man army was to guard the frontier in what had become the increasingly unlikely event of an Indian attack. The country had raised huge armies for the Civil War, but that conflict was only a receding memory. There was no federal income tax and no large federal bureaucracy. Most citizens could go from month to month without directly encountering an agency of the national government in Washington.

The tasks that the government was expected to perform were also minimal. No system of old-age insurance existed. Individuals were expected to rely on family and friends when they could no longer work for themselves. In the same way, when a person was fired or laid-off from a job, there was no provision for unemployment insurance. An individual would have to live off savings or relatives until another position was located. If a disabling injury occurred in the factory or mill, no workmen's compensation program existed to allow the employee time to regain their health. Young children labored in factories and textile mills, often from the age of nine or ten onward, and their work days were ten to twelve hours. For older employees the six-day week and the twelve-hour day were standard in many businesses. The privilege of a vacation was rare, and holidays were few. Almost no effective protections existed for American workers in the emerging industrial society [20 *pp. 42–5*].

Labor unions, which might have been expected to have assisted industrial workers, were only in their infancy. The American Federation of Labor, formed in 1886, embraced members of skilled craft unions, and did not seek to enroll the large body of factory laborers or unskilled employees. The most recent such union, the Knights of Labor, had peaked in 1886 and was four years later only a remnant of what it had been. Effective union power to challenge management was more than a half century in the future.

The conventional wisdom of the society believed that a nation with a weak national government reflected the best possible answers to social concerns. Individuals were seen legally as existing on an equal basis with large corporations. It was not the responsibility of business or of society to help a person who was out of work. Intervening in that predicament would erode the self-reliance and moral character of the person involved.

In 1890, the main mechanism for expressing political attitudes was the well-entrenched two-party system. The Democrats were the older of the two organizations. They traced their roots back to the earliest days of the Republic and the organizing efforts of James Madison and Thomas Jefferson in the 1790s. The Democratic hero was Andrew Jackson, who had brought the party to power in 1828 and had entrenched the principles of small government and state rights in which all Democrats believed. The party was strongest in the South because of the lingering effects of the Civil War and the identification of the Republicans with the Union cause. As one southern Democrat put it, 'no historian will ever find such contradiction in the political world as a Democrat who does not believe in state rights' [21; 28; 39; 53 p. 262].

The Republicans were a younger party. They had burst onto the scene in the 1850s as a way for northerners to express their opposition to slavery and the political power of the South. They also included individuals who thought that national power could be used to enhance the growth of the economy or to make Americans achieve a more godly and devout society. The experience of winning the Civil War was a basic element in the Republican party and its members regarded the Democrats as somehow unpatriotic and disloyal. A Republican senator summed up the party's philosophy: 'One of the highest duties of Government is the adoption of such economic policy as may encourage and develop every industry to which the soil and climate of the country are adapted' [20 p. 190].

In the decades following the war, the Republicans and Democrats had adopted positions very different from the ideological attitudes they would take up during the twentieth century when the Democrats were the party of a powerful central government and the Republicans stood for a smaller, less intrusive government. In broad terms, the late nineteenth-century Republicans were the party of economic nationalism and an activist government to encourage industrial growth. Their main policy commitment was to the protective tariff, which they saw as a way of encouraging business enterprise and providing jobs for American workers. Opposition to Great Britain, the most powerful free trade nation in the world, was another staple of Republican tariff rhetoric.

The Democrats, on the other hand, were the party of limited government, state rights, and localism. They opposed the tariff and high taxation. Democrats saw Americans as consumers who would be adversely affected by higher taxes and an activist government. Neither party as yet believed that government regulation was an appropriate policy.

By 1890, a prolonged stalemate in national politics had become an accepted fact of life for partisan leaders. Since the mid-1870s and the end of Reconstruction, the Republicans and Democrats had battled on even terms with neither one enjoying a clear ascendancy. Presidential elections were decided by very narrow margins. In the most recent contest, pitting Democrat Grover Cleveland against Republican Benjamin Harrison in 1888, for example, Cleveland had won a majority of the popular vote, but had lost to Harrison when the votes of the states in the Electoral College were tabulated. During the two decades from 1872 to 1892, the Democrats usually controlled the House of Representatives and the Republicans had an advantage in the Senate. With divided government went a reluctance to adopt strong policies that might alienate key blocs of voters [49].

After the presidential election of 1888, with the Republicans having elected Benjamin Harrison as president and gained control of both houses of Congress, the deadlock started to break apart. To the Republicans, the moment seemed propitious to enact their economic goals. Using their majorities in the Fifty-First Congress, the Republicans, or the 'Grand Old Party' (GOP) as they called themselves, pushed an activist program that included higher tariffs, the expansion of the currency (the Sherman Silver Purchase Act), and regulation of large corporations (the Sherman Antitrust Act). The Republican leader who pushed this agenda was Speaker Thomas B. Reed of Maine. He used the House rules and the power of the chair to persuade his colleagues to adopt their program of tariff protection, an antitrust statute, and currency legislation. The Republicans hoped that positive program would translate into a permanent majority status [20 *pp. 224–5*].

To their dismay, the Republicans found that their legislative energy in the Fifty-First Congress (1889–90) produced a serious backlash at the polls in the congressional elections of 1890. Using the argument that the Republicans had passed costly tariffs and embarked on a policy of government spending, the Democrats assailed the Republicans as big spenders who had been responsible for the 'Billion Dollar Congress,' the first session to appropriate that much money to run the government. As a result of these appeals, the Democrats regained control of the House of Representatives and made gains in the Senate. In the wake of the setback, the administration of Benjamin Harrison faced serious problems for the president's re-election in 1892. The voters had said no to the Republican effort to use national power to promote economic growth. In the process, the electorate had shaken up the stalemated system and encouraged new ideas.

The 1890 elections saw the rise of a third party from the South and West that would challenge the Democrats and Republicans during the next several years. The People's Party, or the Populists, as they called themselves, grew out of the Depression and low commodity prices that plagued the farm sector at the end of the 1890s. Prices for wheat and cotton had plummeted from the profitable levels of the mid-1880s. Wheat that had brought the farmer nearly $1.20 a bushel in 1881 yielded only $0.70 a bushel eight years later. Cotton experienced similar declines. In the process, the farmers found that the debts they had assumed to start their businesses were now much more of an economic burden. The angry farmers wanted the government to raise crop prices and inflate the currency to make their debts easier to pay. They also called for government control or tighter regulation of railroads and monopolies. While the Populists would not succeed in their crusade, they would be an important force in making more legitimate ideas of increasing governmental power to oversee the economy. Their platform in 1890, for example, called for postal savings banks, a graduated income tax, and the direct election of United States senators [20; 22].

The Populists became participants in the 1892 presidential election when they nominated James B. Weaver as their candidate against the major party contestants. President Harrison sought a second term, although his party was unenthusiastic about his chances. Grover Cleveland received a third consecutive nomination and was favored to win. The Populists denounced the current state of politics in their platform, adopted at their convention in Omaha. Its preamble said that 'we meet in the midst of a nation brought to the verge of moral, political, and material ruin' [*Doc. 1*]. The Populists received more than a million popular votes, but Cleveland easily defeated them and Harrison. He gained 277 electoral votes to Harrison's 145 and Weaver's 22. As a result, Cleveland became the only president to serve two non-consecutive terms.

THE BEGINNINGS OF REFORM

In the early 1890s, other currents of change stirred in the United States. Greater attention focused on the plight of the nation's major cities, where an exploding population and powerful political machines made urban life an urgent social problem. To address the ills of city life, men and women opened 'settlement houses' in the neighborhoods of Chicago and New York. The most famous of these settlements was Hull House, started by Jane Addams and Ellen Starr in 1889. Starr and Addams, and the other settlement workers, lived among the people they were trying to help and brought activities, education, and a sympathetic presence to the neighborhood. Addams would later remark that the settlement movement was 'an attempt to relieve, at the same time, the overaccumulation at one end of society and the destitution at the other.' Other settlement house experiments appeared in New York, Boston, and Philadelphia. From the settlement house experience would emerge a generation of reformers who would pursue crusades for other issues such as limiting the hours of work, inspection of factories, and regulation of public utilities [29 *p. 14*].

Closely linked to the spirit of the settlement house effort at the end of the 1890s was what became known as the Social Gospel. During the 1880s there had been many examples of labor unrest, most notably the Haymarket Riot of 1886 in Chicago, in which a bomb killed policemen and for which anarchists were blamed. The alleged participants were tried, convicted, and sentenced to death. Four men were executed. It seemed for a moment as though European-style anarchy might be gaining a foothold in the new metropolises.

The incident sent shockwaves through respectable circles as a sign of imminent social disruption, but some Protestant and Catholic clergy regarded what had happened as a miscarriage of justice. They believed that city-dwellers had legitimate grievances that the political system was not addressing. They asked themselves how the churches were responding to the needs of working people. Many of the champions of what became known as the Social Gospel decided that Protestantism needed to be more sensitive to the plight of the poor and unfortunate in society. Among the leaders of the movement were Walter Rauschenbusch, who said that the church should be 'the appointed instrument for the further realization of that new society in the world about it' [29 *p. 14*]. Similar attitudes were expressed by Roman Catholic priests and rabbis of Jewish congregations.

The spirit of the Social Gospel spilled over into what became progressivism. The sense that they were doing God's work in the world affected reformers from Jane Addams to Theodore Roosevelt. To some degree there was also condescension in the way that advocates of the Social Gospel sought to uplift the less fortunate without understanding their culture and values. Other reformers saw their movement as a way of forestalling more radical change among the poor and in that way used their doctrines as a form of controlling social unrest. But at their core the Social Gospel and the settlement movement embodied a real sense of concern about the plight of the disadvantaged and the direction of society as industrialism became more prevalent.

Another element in the emerging spirit of reform grew out of changes in American higher education, where academics were questioning the doctrines of limited government that had been part of the orthodoxy of college courses throughout the period after the Civil War. The theory known as *laissez-faire* (or let alone) had important champions, such as William Graham Sumner of Yale University and the British Social Darwinist Herbert Spencer. But as the 1880s proceeded, these principles seemed to younger scholars less and less relevant to the needs of society. Those younger faculty who had studied in Germany, where the state under Otto von Bismarck had created social insurance programs, asked why such answers might not be applied in the United States [42].

New professional organizations dedicated to expanding the role of the state soon appeared. One of these was the American Economic Association, founded in 1885, which said that social problems would need 'the united efforts, each in its own sphere, of the church, the state, and of science' [29 *p. 42*]. The economists, historians, and political scientists who taught these newer ideas in their classrooms during the 1880s and 1890s imbued a generation of their students with the precept that men and women of energy and devotion could create a better world for the people of the United States.

A major catalyst for shaping the reform spirit in the 1890s was the outbreak of the Depression of that decade in 1893. Economic downturns in the United States were called 'panics' before society adopted what seemed to be the less loaded word 'depression.' By any standard, the Panic of 1893 was an economic calamity. Triggered by the failure of some British banking firms, the economic slump hit the United States in the spring of 1893 and lasted for four bitter years. By the end of the year, hundreds of businesses had failed, a quarter of the workforce was unemployed, and hard times fell across the land. As one newspaper wrote, 'money withdrew itself from the channels of trade; mills closed, business became stagnant, uncertainty and fear spread like a pall over a hitherto prosperous land' [39 *pp. 448–9*].

Many middle-class citizens feared that social revolution was imminent. They shuddered when men such as Jacob Coxey of Ohio led an 'army of the unemployed' to Washington to ask for work during the spring of 1894. Coxey's Army moved along from Ohio toward Washington as reporters tramped with the marchers to recount the daily routine. Washington police arrested Coxey on the steps of the Capitol and turned his supporters away, but the fear of what he represented remained.

Even more disturbing to middle-class Americans was the nationwide Pullman Strike that erupted a few months later. When Eugene V. Debs and the American Railway Union called a sympathetic boycott to help the striking workers in Pullman, Illinois, the Cleveland administration sent in troops to maintain order in Chicago and the surrounding area. The workers were no match for the troops, and Cleveland's stand for law and order won him some temporary support. Other citizens noted, however, that the workers in the model town of Pullman had walked out after George M. Pullman, the builder of luxury railroad cars, had cut wages and kept his rents high during the worst of the Depression. The episode made Cleveland seem unsympathetic to the desperate plight of the unemployed [49].

THE REALIGNING ELECTION OF 1894

In national politics, the big losers from the Panic were the Democrats because of President Grover Cleveland's inability to develop a program to relieve suffering and to respond to the downturn. In 1893 the president summoned Congress into special session to repeal the Sherman Silver Purchase Act of 1890, which had provided some financial support for silver producers. Cleveland got his way, but at the cost of a broken Democratic party. Throughout 1894 the administration stumbled from crisis to crisis. The promises of tariff reform in 1892 became the unpopular Wilson–Gorman Tariff of 1894, which actually raised rates on some products. A disgusted Cleveland let the measure become law without his signature. The Democrats went into the 1894 elections divided and demoralized.

The president's apparent insensitivity to the suffering of the poor drove voters toward the Republicans and to a lesser degree toward the Populists. Soon the Democrats were split between their inflationary wing that favored the free and unlimited coinage of silver into money at a fixed ratio with gold and the champions of the gold standard. The free silver forces were from the South and West; the goldbugs, as they were known, lived in the Northeast and urban Middle West. The silver issue triggered a battle among Democrats that became almost a crusade for partisans of either the yellow metal or its silver counterpart.

The Populists hoped to inherit the protest vote against the Depression from the Democrats, but that did not prove to be the case. The inflationary answers that they proposed had little appeal outside of the farm belt. Industrial workers on fixed incomes saw little merit in free silver that would raise prices on the goods they had to buy. As a result, the Populists remained confined to their regional base. In the South, moreover, the Democrats used their control of the election machinery to beat back the Populist challenge. People's Party candidates were counted out at the ballot box and their voters intimidated from casting a vote through violence.

The beneficiaries of the unhappiness with the economy were the Republicans, and they made huge gains in the congressional elections of 1894. They united behind the doctrine that the country needed higher tariffs to see a return of prosperity, and they fought the election in that spirit. One of their leading orators was the governor of Ohio, William McKinley, who toured the Middle West, making 371 speeches on behalf of his party's candidates. Former Speaker of the House Thomas B. Reed predicted that the 'Democratic dead will be so numerous that they will be buried in a common grave and marked unknown' [39 *p. 477*].

It was almost that decisive a victory for the Grand Old Party. In the largest transfer of congressional seats from one party to another in the nation's history, the Republicans picked up 113 seats while the Democrats saw 116 of their members go down to defeat. In large parts of the Middle West, the Democrats essentially disappeared as an electoral presence.

The key impact of the 1894 election was more enduring. It meant that the deadlocked politics of the 1880s were over, and the Republicans were clearly established as the majority party in the North and Middle West. The Democrats were relegated to their base in the South and a presence in the Rocky Mountain West where silver sentiment was strong. One central element in the emergence of the progressive spirit was Republican dominance, which made younger politicians restive for a chance to prove themselves and eager to embrace newer ideas.

THE VARIETIES OF REFORM

While the Republicans were taking control of national affairs in the 1894 election, another response to the Depression was occurring on the local and state levels. As the hard times hit the middle classes in states such as Wisconsin and Michigan, concerned citizens began to organize to protest high taxes, the power of public utilities, and political corruption. These groups had different names, but their underlying purposes were the same. There was the Municipal Franchise League of Boston, Massachusetts, the Civic Federation in Chicago, the New York Consumers' League, and the Boss Busters League in Kansas. Each of them addressed perceived inequities in how their city or state operated, and proposed greater authority for non-partisan organizations to offset the rule of the major parties. In each instance, there was an explicit or implicit call for a greater role for local and state government in overseeing the economy [29].

The 1890s saw ferment spill out into all sections of society. Influential exposés of major industries such as Henry Demarest Lloyd's *Wealth Against Commonwealth* (1894) examined the monopolistic tactics of Standard Oil and John D. Rockefeller. In the cities, reformers went into the tenements and the factories to reveal the conditions of the poor in work such as Jacob Riis's study *How the Other Half Lives* (1890). 'Say what you will,' observed Riis, 'a man cannot live like a pig and vote like a man' [45 *p. 248*].

Here and there specific examples of what city government could do appeared. Residents of Detroit had elected a businessman named Hazen Pingree as their mayor in 1889. In his early years in office, he was a conventional performer who provided the efficient services his platform had advocated. But Pingree changed as circumstances shifted. He came out against the power of the gas and electric utilities. The Depression moved him even more toward innovative solutions to poverty. He allocated vacant lots to those out of work so they could grow their own food. He reallocated taxes onto the more affluent. The Republican party in Michigan repudiated him but Pingree pressed ahead. Eventually he was elected governor of Michigan in 1897 [29; 45; 59].

Another reform enclave was Toledo, Ohio, where Samuel L. 'Golden Rule' Jones served as mayor from 1897 to 1905. A self-made success in selling oil-drilling supplies, Jones was put forward as a candidate for mayor. In city hall, Jones advocated that the government use its power to erect playgrounds for the young, a place for the homeless to live, and city-sponsored recreation facilities for all of Toledo's people. Jones also pressed for city control of the utilities that served the entire population. Conservatives attacked men such as Pingree and Jones, but their example attracted reformers from across the country to emulate what had been achieved in Detroit and Toledo [45].

A significant element in the gathering momentum for reform was the role of women. Their participation in politics was limited because of their inability to vote, but they made their influence felt in other ways. One important avenue for women was the club movement, led by the General Federation of Women's Clubs, which contended that the country needed the humanizing effect of women in civic life. 'Municipal housekeeping' would make cities cleaner and more efficient. Women also became staunch advocates of what a later generation would call environmentalism. They provided the energy and drive for such organizations as the Sierra Club and the Audubon Society. Their concern for the welfare of children also spurred the creation of juvenile courts for young people who ran afoul of the law [89; 92].

The effort to obtain the vote for women also picked up some momentum during the first half of the 1890s. Divided since the aftermath of the Civil War, the American Woman Suffrage Association and the National Woman Suffrage Association decided to join forces in 1890 under the name of the National American Woman Suffrage Association (NAWSA). Five years later a new leader appeared for the cause in the person of Carrie Chapman Catt, who set about organizing state branches, creating local clubs, and pursuing her goal that 'the opening of the twentieth century would find our entire people all aglow with the woman suffrage movement' [93 *p. 8*]. Despite Catt's energy, that goal remained elusive during the remainder of the decade, but she was laying the foundation for future successes.

Other reforms that would become part of the progressive agenda were the subject of new methods during the 1890s as well. The campaign to restrict the sale and use of alcoholic beverages had long been part of the American scene, but the prohibitionist drive was largely stalled during the 1890s. The Woman's Christian Temperance Union (WCTU), founded in the 1870s, had become a pervasive presence in national politics during the ensuing twenty years. Its leader, Frances Willard, was recognized as one of the most effective lobbyists in the nation. However, the progress of the reform was slow, and restive prohibitionists (drys) wanted a more effective plan of action.

In 1895 the Anti-Saloon League was launched from Westerville, Ohio. Its goal was not to transform the drinker, but to eliminate the places where drinks were served. A forerunner of a modern lobbying interest, the League pushed clear, limited goals to reduce the political influence of drink in state after state. Methodically, it tried to make counties and cities liquor-free. Then it would move to the state level, and its ultimate goal was national legislation to make the sale of liquor illegal. It labeled the liquor lobby a special interest that corrupted politics, and it used similar language to make the same case for pure elections, clean government, and the removal of malign influences, as did those who assailed corporate power. The case of alcohol reform in the United States illustrates that not all social changes that were advocated would impress later generations as appropriate reform goals [99].

That was certainly also true of the effort to restrict immigration into the United States. The flow of newcomers into the United States was steady during the depression years of the decade. By 1900 there were 11 million foreign-born citizens, and this fact produced organizations whose goal it was to slow down or cut off the tide of immigration. The Immigration Restriction League, based in Massachusetts, had among its adherents Senator Henry Cabot Lodge of that state. He and like-minded colleagues sponsored laws that would have required immigrants to take and pass a literacy test before being allowed to enter the country. President Cleveland vetoed such a measure in 1897 just before he left office [20].

Immigration restriction and prohibition illustrated some of the cultural ambiguities of reform in the United States. There was a degree of social control and political coercion behind some of the progressive rhetoric. The power of the state could be used in ways that diminished tolerance and diversity to achieve the goal of a racially purer and more homogeneous society. Reform was not a self-defining concept or one that insured the social virtue of whoever identified with change.

THE SEGREGATED SOUTH

A striking example of this aspect of reform involved the situation of African Americans in the United States. For them, 1896 marked a year in which the United States Supreme Court put a judicial stamp of endorsement on a system of race relations in the South that made them second-class citizens in their own country. For many white southerners, the development of segregation in the 1890s went forward as a 'reform' of the existing structure of race relations. Following the Civil War and Reconstruction, there had been a period of fluidity in which blacks and whites had interacted with some freedom in southern politics and daily life [16; 74].

By the early 1890s, however, the situation of southern race relations began to change as whites asserted control over politics, economics, and culture toward black citizens. In public life, the instruments of white dominance included the white primary in which potential voters had to swear that they were white Democrats, the poll tax where a payment for voting was demanded, and the literacy test that compelled illiterate black and white voters to answer questions before being handed a ballot. When these techniques did not reduce the black electorate quickly enough, election fraud and violence came into play to insure that African Americans did not vote or hold office. During the period 1882–89 more than 2,500 black men and women were the victims of lynchings [16; 76; 77].

In daily life, the customs of segregation pervaded the existence of African Americans in the South. They had to endure second-class segregated facilities in schools, railroad trains, and public accommodations. As one white put it, 'After all, it is not important which end of the car is given to the nigger. The main point is that he must sit where he is told' [74 *p. 232*]. Courtesy titles were reserved for whites. A wrong glance, a disrespectful answer to a question, or even just white irritation at some imagined slight could provoke violence and death. As for educating African Americans, many southern whites believed that it was pointless to do so. An Alabama lawyer said: 'If you educate the Negroes they won't stay where they belong; and you must consider them as a race, because if you let a few rise it makes the others discontented' [74 *p. 95*].

In the mid-1890s, blacks looked to a national leader named Booker T. Washington, who urged them to accept segregation as an inescapable fact of life. He delivered a famous speech at the Cotton States Exposition in Atlanta in 1895 in which he urged his fellow African Americans to 'suffer in silence' [74 *p. 354*]. Whites applauded Washington's sentiments, which tended to support the existing system of race relations. Behind the scenes Washington worked through the courts to undermine segregation, but his public image remained one of deference to white dominance.

A challenge to segregation had worked its way through the nation's courts and finally reached the Supreme Court in 1896. Homer Adolph Plessy was a black man in Louisiana who had refused to ride in the railroad car set aside for members of his race. Instead, he had sued the state of Louisiana on the grounds that segregation violated his rights under the Fourteenth Amendment. In the majority decision, Justice Henry Billings Brown of Massachusetts argued that segregation did not violate the rights of black Americans under the Thirteenth and Fourteenth Amendments. Separate but equal practices, institutions, and services would be constitutional. He added that segregation would represent a 'badge of inferiority' if 'the colored race chooses to put that construction on it.' A vigorous dissent by Justice John Marshall Harlan said that 'our Constitution is color-blind and neither knows nor tolerates classes among citizens.' The practical effect of the decision was to validate segregation laws and to encourage their spread throughout the South [*Doc. 3*; 20 *p. 153*].

MCKINLEY VERSUS BRYAN IN 1896

In national politics the presidential election of 1896 brought the final repudiation of the Democrats and the electoral triumph of the Republicans that the 1894 congressional elections had forecast. The Republican candidate was William McKinley, who had established himself as the front-runner by the early months of 1896. A Civil War veteran, McKinley had established himself as a champion of the protective tariff in Congress from 1876 to 1890. His ability to carry Ohio in two gubernatorial races, his identification with the tariff, and his popularity within the party enabled him to triumph over the other Republican candidates. His campaign benefited from the organizational talents of the Cleveland industrialist Marcus Alonzo 'Mark' Hanna, but McKinley was the architect of his own success. He won on the first ballot and expected to make the main issues of his campaign the protective tariff and the return of prosperity after four years of Democratic hard times [64].

In a surprise, however, the Democrats chose a political unknown to lead their party. By 1896 the anti-Cleveland forces within the party had gained the lead over their rivals and were on their way to making free silver their rallying cry. At the Democratic Convention in Chicago, the Cleveland men were brushed aside in favor of those who wanted inflation and free silver. There was a bitter debate about the party's platform and the party's stance on silver. One of the participants in the debate was a 36-year-old Nebraskan named William Jennings Bryan. He had served two terms in Congress from Nebraska, and then had perfected his oratory in numerous appearances before Democratic audiences during 1895 and early 1896. Bryan told his friends that he would be nominated in 1896 because he best represented the attitudes of his party toward free silver. During the platform debate, Bryan delivered an impassioned speech on behalf of silver. The audience in the hall listened enthralled as he denounced the advocates of gold and spoke of the virtues of silver. Bryan ended with the phrase 'Thou shalt not crucify mankind upon a Cross of Gold' as he spread his arms wide like a man crucified for his beliefs. So compelling was Bryan's oratory and so eager was his party for a champion of silver that the Democrats nominated him the next day [*Doc. 2; 21 p. 121*].

The Populists had expected both major parties to select a candidate pledged to the gold standard. Bryan's emergence left them without a workable strategy. They had no choice but to accept Bryan as their nominee too, lest the silver forces be split. The rationale for a third party evaporated when they did so. The Populists had imparted fresh ideas about a more active, regulatory government, and they had shaken the two-party system. Their inability to move beyond their base in the South and West meant that they could not solve the dilemma of third parties in the United States. Replacing one of the two major parties required a national presence, and that the Populists could not achieve. After the election, however, they gradually disappeared as prosperity returned to the farm belt [49].

The campaign between Bryan and McKinley aroused the American electorate as have few campaigns before or since. In the North over 75 percent of eligible voters went to the polls. Bryan went out making speeches on his own as a forerunner of the modern style of American campaigns.

Without much money at his disposal, he had to rely on his own personality and oratory to carry him to victory. Starting with a rush in the days after his nomination, he seemed to be in the lead as August turned into September. Crowds packed in to see him as he crossed the nation on a railroad car addressing audiences at towns large and small.

McKinley and his advisers decided 'This is a year for press and pen.' They raised campaign money from large corporations, perhaps $4 million (around $50 or 60 million in today's terms), and they poured it into several hundred million pamphlets and newspaper advertisements. Meanwhile, McKinley stayed at his home in Canton, Ohio, and addressed the crowds that gathered near his front porch. Some 750,000 people came to listen to McKinley in September and October. Each day the Republican candidate made brief, effective speeches that the newspapers reported around the country. McKinley and the Republicans understood that the campaign had to stay 'on message' (a phrase of modern political consultants) and they did so with impressive efficiency. Over and over McKinley stressed that free silver would decrease the value of the dollar and cost jobs for workers. Gradually the tide for Bryan ebbed and then reversed itself. By the eve of the election it was clear that McKinley was going to win [64 *p. 11*].

The election results confirmed the forecasts. McKinley had a 600,000-vote lead in the popular vote totals, the largest margin since the election of 1872 when Ulysses S. Grant defeated Horace Greeley. In the electoral result, the outcome was equally decisive. McKinley had 271 electoral votes to 176 for Bryan. The McKinley victory confirmed what had happened in 1894 and ushered in a prolonged period of Republican dominance of American politics.

The 1896 election also marked another key turning point in national politics that would shape the progressive reform campaign. The high turn-out and intense partisanship of the McKinley–Bryan contest soon faded. McKinley and Hanna had placed less reliance on the Republican party machinery and had conducted their own campaign. The emphasis on political literature and educating the informed voter meant that partisan techniques such as the rallies, clubs, and marches of the 1880s were no longer crucial. By devaluing the party, the need for voters to have a strong commitment to the Republicans or Democrats came into question. Some of the intensity and passion went out of American politics after 1896, and in their places came the non-partisan reform measures identified with progressivism.

Bryan's success in gaining the Democratic nomination at the age of thirty-six also showed that it was possible for a young outsider to leap over traditional practices and attain national leadership. At the same time, the Nebraskan infused his party with an anti-corporate, pro-regulation spirit that would carry the Democrats away from their earlier negative attitude toward governmental power. The commitment of the South to state rights and racial segregation meant that Democratic endorsement of a strong government could go only so far. But what Bryan had started grew in importance before 1914.

Historians have long puzzled about why the United States did not erupt in social violence or more radical political change during the economic upheavals of the 1890s. To some extent there was a high degree of unrest, as such episodes as the march of Jacob Coxey on Washington or the Pullman Strike attested. Yet, despite all the misery that attended the economic problems of the first half of the 1890s, citizens still retained a faith that the system could be changed by peaceful means. Moderate reform could stave off more sweeping alterations in the country. That faith would animate the progressive spirit that gathered strength in the years after McKinley entered the White House as the twenty-fifth president on 4 March, 1897.

PART TWO   ANALYSIS

CHAPTER TWO

PROGRESSIVISM EMERGENT

The years from 1897 to 1902 are not generally regarded as part of the true period of progressivism. With William McKinley in the White House until 1901 and the war with Spain under way in 1898, this period is usually seen as a conservative moment before the flamboyant Theodore Roosevelt entered the national scene. In fact, however, this impression is misleading. The second half of the 1890s saw a number of important developments that would contribute to the reform impulse. Among the most significant of these changes was the rise of trusts and holding companies once the Depression of the 1890s had passed. A second element was the Spanish–American War and the debate over imperialism that ensued from the brief conflict. Finally, in the cities and states, a generation of reform politicians arrived at the threshold of national prominence. Such individuals as Theodore Roosevelt and Robert M. La Follette settled into the roles that they would play for the next decade and a half.

The most significant aspect of the years after 1896 was the return of prosperity following the four years of depression. Gold discoveries in South Africa and the Canadian Yukon ended the shortage of currency that had worsened the deflation of the first half of the 1890s. With more money in circulation, consumer prices rose and wages followed suit, although at a slower rate. The good times that followed lasted through the outbreak of World War I. One central fact of the progressive movement was that it occurred during a time of prosperity when Americans felt that it was possible to make changes in their society without risking their economic future.

In fact, the whole period before 1914 was suffused with a confidence about the direction of history that now seems quaint and at odds with the violent and bloody record that the twentieth century provided. Americans during the Progressive Era were on the other side of the great cataclysm of World War I that did so much to destroy the optimism and self-confidence of the early twentieth century. In that period when Europe had not known a general war for a century, the possibility that major bloodletting might occur seemed remote.

As the economic scene brightened, Americans could envision a future of expanding growth and greater social harmony. The nation's problems seemed manageable and open to satisfactory resolution. Progressives especially believed that human nature was basically good and that government could improve and perfect society to create a better world. Many individuals spoke of the years before 1914 as a time of optimism and hope when it seemed possible to bring the better world into reality. As Ray Stannard Baker, one of the 'muckraking' journalists of the period, wrote in his memoirs, 'We "muckraked" not because we hated our world but because we loved it. We were not hopeless, we were not cynical, we were not bitter' [31 *p. 195*].

THE WAR WITH SPAIN AND ITS CONSEQUENCES

This sense of possibility and purpose gained momentum from the emergence of the United States as a world power in 1898. For three years the nation had watched the bloody and prolonged rebellion against Spanish rule that had been going on in the nearby island of Cuba. President Grover Cleveland had followed a pro-Spanish policy until his term ended in March 1897. William McKinley came into office hoping for a negotiated solution to the uprising, but unwilling to impose a settlement that the Cuban rebels would not accept. Since the only terms to which the Cubans would agree included independence from Spain, a negotiated settlement between the two sides was unlikely. During 1897 the McKinley administration tried to nudge Spain toward a voluntary departure from the island without success. For Spain, giving up Cuba without a struggle was equivalent to ceding a part of the Spanish homeland [64].

Early in 1898 matters took a more ominous turn. Negotiations in January and February revealed the gulf between the two nations over the fate of Cuba. Then on 15 February 1898 the battleship *USS Maine* exploded in Havana harbor killing more than 270 officers and men. American public opinion clamored for intervention to avenge the dead from the *Maine*, to punish the Spanish for their conduct in Cuba, and to extend American dominance in the Caribbean. Under intense pressure from a warlike Congress, the McKinley administration intensified negotiations with Madrid for a peaceful settlement, but the gulf between the two nations could not be bridged. By April the United States and Spain were at war, and three months later what John Hay called a 'splendid little war' had ended in complete victory for the United States [31 *p. 164*].

In the armistice that brought hostilities to a close, the United States left open the possibility that the Philippine Islands might become part of the new American empire. The domestic political issue then arose of whether it would be wise for the nation to acquire the Philippine Islands from Spain as a permanent American possession. The McKinley administration believed that such a policy was justified, and the president used the powers of his office to persuade Congress to agree. He went out on a speaking tour in the autumn of 1898 to rouse popular support for expansionism. It marked one of McKinley's innovative uses of presidential power.

The debate over imperialism that ensued pitted advocates of expansion against the anti-imperialists. The proponents of empire included such figures as Senator Henry Cabot Lodge of Massachusetts, Theodore Roosevelt, and Senator Albert J. Beveridge of Indiana. They asserted that the United States had to become a world power to meet the challenge of competition from aggressive European powers such as France, Germany, and Great Britain. If the United States failed to compete in the international arena, imperialists argued, it would become a second-rate power subject to the whims of stronger countries. There was also a significant component of racial superiority in American imperialism. As Beveridge put it, the Lord had rendered Americans 'adept in government that we may administer government among savage and senile peoples' [20 *p. 265*]. As long as conquest was easy and the obligations of imperialism slight, many citizens found the adventure of empire an appealing experience.

On the other side of the case were those who argued that adding the Philippines and other overseas possessions would mark a fundamental break with the traditional values of the country. Led by Andrew Carnegie, Thomas B. Reed, and Carl Schurz, the Anti-Imperialist League sought to rally public opinion against overseas expansion. Carl Schurz spoke for many of them when he said in January 1899: 'I deny that the liberation of those Spanish dependencies morally constrains us to do anything that would put our highest mission to solve the great problem of democratic government in jeopardy, or that would otherwise endanger the vital interests of the republic' [*Doc. 4*].

Anti-imperialists charged that American institutions could not be imperialistic and democratic at the same time. Involvement in European rivalries would make war more likely. Some anti-imperialists turned racial prejudice on its head and asserted that adding Latin American or Asian possessions would bring inferior peoples under the nation's sovereignty. While the anti-imperialists lost the short-run argument and could not prevent the ratification of the peace treaty, many of their contentions resonated with the public once the prolonged conflict with the Filipinos began in 1899. For the moment, however, President McKinley spoke for his fellow citizens when he said in February 1899 that 'No imperial designs lurk in the American mind. They are alien to American sentiment, thought, and purpose. Our priceless principles undergo no change under a tropical sun. They go with the flag' [*Doc. 5*].

The outcome of the debate regarding the treaty ended in victory for the McKinley administration. The president wielded the power of patronage and White House influence to sway undecided Democrats. Bryan helped too when he argued that his party should approve the treaty and make imperialism an issue in the 1900 elections. In February 1899, the Senate endorsed the document by one vote more than the necessary two-thirds. At the same time, Filipino nationalists resisted the American presence and fighting broke out between the two sides. The war that resulted proved to be a difficult and dirty one for the American forces. Soldiers resorted to torture and other harsh practices as the Filipinos turned to guerrilla warfare to oust the invaders. The United States found itself using some of the same cruel policies toward the Filipinos that it had condemned when Spain employed them in Cuba a few years earlier. The protracted fighting cooled American enthusiasm for additional imperialism as reports of atrocities filled the newspapers [45].

As the debate continued, however, critics of American policy pointed to examples of cruel behavior toward the Cubans and the Filipinos where the United States fell short of its own professed ideals. Henry Van Dyke, a Presbyterian pastor in New York City, said that 'when imperialism comes in at the door democracy flies out the window.' A Populist legislator from South Dakota asked 'What kind of "blessings of law and liberty" is it that we are going to extend to the people of these islands? Is it the same kind which these same "expansionists" are now extending to our own laboring classes?' [22 *pp. 148, 152*]. Imperialists countered that the United States was extending the blessings of democracy to peoples that had not known that kind of rule in the past. Despite the intensity that the advocates of expansion brought to their cause, the costs of overseas adventures in human and financial terms ate away at the desire for additional possessions.

THE 1900 PRESIDENTIAL ELECTION

The debate over imperialism became one of the major issues in the presidential election of 1900 that once again pitted Bryan versus McKinley. Finding that the issue of free silver that had galvanized his campaign four years earlier was no longer a rallying point for Democrats, Bryan turned to the question of expansionism as an early theme of his race for the White House. The Democratic platform asserted that overseas imperialism 'growing out of the Spanish war, involves the very existence of the Republican, and the destruction of our free institutions. We regard it as the paramount issue of the campaign.' Bryan said that the United States should grant the Philippines independence and then establish an American protectorate over the islands to safeguard them against European or Asian interference [64 *p. 220*].

To this approach, McKinley and the Republicans countered that such an arrangement would insure American involvement with other nations in Asia and Europe and would not provide for effective government in the Philippines. The president got the better of the debate. Few Americans wanted to abandon the gains of the war or leave the Philippines to their own fate. Bryan began to play down imperialism as the campaign progressed. He returned to the tested issue of free silver, and also assailed McKinley and his party over the issue of big business and the trusts [64].

Yet the continuing war in the Philippines and the tactics that the United States Army used to suppress the nationalist rebels left American public opinion ill-disposed to take on further imperialist responsibilities. Thus, while the anti-imperialists lost the debate about the direction the nation should take in foreign policy, their comments did cause their fellow citizens to draw back from the full implications of an expansionist policy. Their criticisms also fostered a rethinking of American ideals as the century ended that made it possible for others to urge that national institutions be re-examined and reformed [28; 45].

The election of 1900 ended in a decisive victory for McKinley and his party. The ticket of McKinley and Theodore Roosevelt had 7,200,000 popular votes to 6,356,000 for Bryan and his running mate, Adlai E. Stevenson. McKinley's success in the electoral college was 292 to 155. The president ran better than he had in 1896, and could boast after the contest that he was 'now President of the whole people.' Republican dominance of national politics was an accomplished fact [64 *p. 230*].

THE TRUST PROBLEM

A second critical development during the second half of the 1890s was the explosive growth of big business. During the Depression, investment bankers such as J.P. Morgan had begun to consolidate railroads and other firms to make them run more efficiently. Morgan insisted on cost-cutting measures, efficient operations, and an absence of labor unrest in his zeal to produce profits. Holding companies were created to own stock in a number of firms and to operate them in the interests of their corporate managers. This process continued once prosperity returned in mid-1897. A number of economic trends made the growth of bigness happen. In New York the emergence of a market for industrial securities enabled capitalists to raise the large amounts of money needed to fund mergers and takeovers. For the seven years after 1897, more than 4,200 companies in the United States turned into 257 corporations. An ominous pattern seemed to be developing in which the opportunity of smaller entrepreneurs was put at risk. 'I do not divide monopolies in private hands into good monopolies and bad monopolies,' said William Jennings Bryan in 1899. 'There is no good monopoly in private hands' [72; 85; *p. 336*].

The critics of the large corporations did not see that bigness was not the universal answer to the challenges that industries faced. Success in the marketplace depended on finding an industry where the methods of production facilitated economies of scale. Where those conditions did not exist the trust movement and holding companies did not gain dominance. But few Americans made these fine economic distinctions between 1897 and 1901. Instead, they saw a steady flow of newspaper announcements about how big business was getting ever bigger [81].

The most striking of these events was the creation of United States Steel in 1901. When Andrew Carnegie sold out his interest to J.P. Morgan, a huge steel combination emerged that was capitalized at $1.4 billion in March 1901. Carnegie himself walked away with $500 million, a huge fortune at a time when income taxes did not exist. This occurred when the nation's gross national product stood at nearly $37 billion. Later in the same year a well-publicized railroad merger produced the Northern Securities Company, a firm that brought together rail lines in the Pacific Northwest. The big corporate names – J.P. Morgan, E.H. Harriman, and James J. Hill – were behind the railroad combine. Smaller businessmen, workers, and the public in general asked about the place of individual Americans in the new world of corporate power. 'The growing antagonism to the concentration of capital,' as one newspaper put it in March 1901, might in time 'lead to one of the greatest social and political upheavals that has been witnessed in modern history' [65 *p. 28*].

In response to these trends, currents of protest and reform stirred in the years preceding the turn of the century. Seven hundred delegates gathered for a conference on the trust problem in Chicago in September 1899. William Jennings Bryan and Michigan governor Hazen Pingree were among those who denounced the trend toward bigness. 'Trusts and monopolies and their defenders stand for special privileges for the few, and unequal opportunities for the many,' said one speaker at the meeting. Several months later another conference met on the same topic and called for more vigorous enforcement of the Sherman Act. That measure had become largely a dead letter as a result of Court decisions in the 1890s that limited the power of the federal government to sue possible monopolies [85 *p. 337*].

THE STATES RESPOND

The suspicion of corporate influence made itself felt in the rise of state politicians who would later become leaders in the progressive moment. In Wisconsin, Robert M. La Follette had broken with the existing leadership of his state's party in the mid-1890s. He ran several races for governor against the Republican power structure without success. After 1897 he began building his appeal on the arguments that local reformers had advanced in response to the Depression, most notably taxation of utilities and the need for direct primaries to select candidates for public office. In 1900, with his victory likely, he and his adversaries reached a truce that enabled him to win the statehouse. The uneasy alliance would soon break down [58; 59].

Another politician who made the issue of trusts a centerpiece of his official duties was Theodore Roosevelt in New York State. The charismatic Roosevelt had won election as governor in 1898 following his battlefield performance in the Spanish–American War. He led his Rough Riders up Kettle Hill against the Spanish positions and became a national hero. Beleaguered Republicans in New York, facing a tough election, nominated him in the fall of 1898 and he won a narrow victory. Even then Roosevelt had his eye on the White House, and he saw New York as a good testing-ground for ideas that might make him a national candidate for the Republicans in 1904.

In office, Roosevelt proved an activist state executive. He held daily press conferences, and consulted experts for proposals about how to deal with consolidated corporate power. He advanced the idea that publicity about the operations of large corporations was the best way to insure their socially beneficial behavior. Roosevelt took this view because he was 'exceedingly alarmed at the growth of popular unrest and popular distrust on this question.' Even his relatively mild idea of providing greater information aroused the suspicions of the leaders of the Republican party. They decided that Roosevelt would be safer as vice president, and in 1900 he was 'kicked upstairs' when the party picked him as William McKinley's running mate. Roosevelt's activism on the state level, however, offered reformers in other states a model of what might be done [3 *vol. II, p. 1045*].

Throughout the waning years of the nineteenth century, movements for reform appeared in many other states. In Iowa, the faction of the Republican party led by Albert Baird Cummins argued that tariff rates should be lowered on goods that trusts produced. Cummins and his allies noted that trusts often sold their goods for less overseas, and thus clearly did not need the protection that the tariff afforded. Their strategy of reducing tariff rates on trust-made products became known as 'The Iowa Idea.' In Kansas, a 'Boss-Busters League' appeared to contest for control of the Republican machinery and to campaign for regulation of railroad rates in the Middle West. On the West Coast, Republicans and Democrats joined in a drive to curb the power of the Southern Pacific Railroad in that state's political life [24 *pp. 26–7*].

The drive for control of the trusts reached such intensity during these years that even President McKinley considered possible programs to provide a greater degree of supervision. He shared Roosevelt's idea that publicity was a useful weapon for the government, and in his mind a distinction was growing between corporations that performed socially useful functions (the so-called 'good' trusts) and businesses that were engaged in predatory practices in the marketplace ('bad' trusts). There was some evidence that McKinley was thinking about antitrust action against the Northern Securities Company before he was assassinated in September 1901. He hoped that gradual reductions in tariff rates through trade treaties with other countries might reduce some of the pressures against the protective system and the perception that big business used the tariff for its selfish purposes [64].

MUCKRAKING REPORTERS

Another important element in the rise of reform sentiment around 1900 was the appearance of what Theodore Roosevelt later called 'muckraking' journalism. By the end of the 1890s an American reader had access to dozens of weekly and monthly magazines that dealt with a dazzling variety of subjects and issues. In 1899 there were more than 1,600 daily newspapers published in the United States. New technology made possible the inexpensive printing of lavishly illustrated periodicals. The audience for these journals expanded rapidly since their cost was low, often as little as 10¢ an issue. The more successful examples of this new form of mass entertainment sold hundreds of thousands of issues.

While many of these publications featured historical topics, romantic stories, and general advice, several publishers saw a possible market in articles that addressed concerns of the time. One of the more visionary publishers was Samuel S. McClure, who operated *McClure's Magazine*. He ran historical works about Lincoln and Napoleon, published such writers as O. Henry and Stephen Crane, and seemed to have a sure sense of what the public wanted to know and read about.

By the turn of the century, McClure recognized that public concern with trusts, the corruption of politics, and the inner workings of government offered a natural field for his staff of talented reporters. He assigned two of his most gifted journalists to look at how trusts worked and how municipal politics operated. To deal with the trusts, he directed Ida Tarbell, who had written about Napoleon, to delve into the Standard Oil Company of John D. Rockefeller. Tarbell's father had seen his own oil business fail because of the ruthless tactics of Rockefeller's company, and she brought passion to her research. She produced a penetrating series about the ways in which Rockefeller had stifled his competitors, broken the law, and extracted concessions from railroads to build up his company. Her history of Standard Oil, though far from objective, confirmed what many Americans thought about the oil company.

Equally graphic and revealing were the stories that another reporter, Lincoln Steffens, wrote about municipal corruption under the title 'The Shame of the Cities.' He went into such major cities as Minneapolis and St Louis, and probed the corrupt links between businesses and the political machines that operated city government. A seasoned reporter who had covered New York City and its complex politics, Steffens recorded how the city officials and their business allies cooperated for their mutual benefit. His articles began appearing in *McClure's* in 1901 and 1902 and they caused a great deal of popular interest in the way that city government worked or didn't work for the benefit of its constituents. As an early student of investigative journalism noted, these reporters also 'drew a new cast of characters for the drama of American society' [31 *p. 197*].

REFORM IN THE CITIES

At the same time that these reporters probed into the weaknesses of city and state government, alternative answers to the traditional forms of city governance were appearing. Galveston, Texas, experienced a devastating hurricane and flood in September 1900 that left the coastal city in ruins and its government out of business. As the residents rebuilt, they turned to ideas of governmental reform that had been discussed in the city during the preceding decade. The state legislature authorized Galveston to dispense with its mayor/city council form of government in which representatives were elected from specific geographic districts. Instead, Galveston set up a five-member commission to run the city. Each commissioner was in charge of one of the key departments in the city such as fire, police, utilities, and housing. The idea was that city affairs could be administered along business-like, non-partisan lines without the rancor and inefficiency that had characterized Galveston politics [89].

The 'Galveston Plan,' as it was called, grew in popularity as the city rebuilt and became prosperous. The reform idea that the commission government model represented had much appeal. It seemed to offer a chance to depart from the older style politics of neighborhoods and partisanship. In their place would come the streamlined efficiency of the corporation with wise, trained commissioners making decisions for the entire city. A variation of this approach was to place the affairs of the town or city in the hands of a city manager who could run a municipality in the way that a chief executive might operate a corporation [88; 90].

There was, however, a drawback to this attractive reform. By shifting power away from the individual neighborhoods and elected representatives, it meant that the business elite and the more affluent sectors of a municipality could exercise greater influence on city affairs. The poor and less powerful found themselves with less of a voice in how they were governed.

The tension between the desire for efficiency and the claims of democratic government would be a continuing source of strain in the progressive movement [107].

THE ADVENT OF THEODORE ROOSEVELT

As 1901 began it seemed as though the United States would continue in the political patterns that President McKinley and the Republicans had established. In the summer the president announced that he would not be a candidate for a third term in 1904, in observance of a two-term tradition for American presidents that had been in existence since the days of George Washington a century earlier.

Instead, McKinley intended to push Congress to take up a program of trade reciprocity that would open up foreign markets for the United States and relieve some of the mounting pressure for reform of the protective tariff. Linking the tariff to trusts, as the Iowa Idea did, for example, attacked the Republicans at their weakest point, and McKinley saw trade treaties as a way to offset these political difficulties without dismantling the system of tariff protection for which the Republicans had fought so long.

The president began his campaign at the Pan-American Exposition in Buffalo, New York, in September 1901. In a speech on September 5, he maintained that the United States could no longer remain aloof from world affairs. 'The period of exclusiveness is past. The expansion of our trade and commerce is the pressing problem,' he said, as he spoke out on behalf of lowering trade barriers [64 *p. 251*].

Had McKinley lived, it is probable that something like the progressive movement would still have emerged in the United States. Whether it would have taken a less divisive form or come later in the first decade of the twentieth century is, of course, impossible to state. The president would probably have done something about the trusts in a less vigorous way than his successor. Nonetheless, the responsibility did not fall to McKinley. On 6 September 1901, standing in line at a reception, he was shot by an anarchist named Leon Czolgosz and died eight days later. At the outset of the twentieth century, presidents were not guarded as closely as they would be a century later. McKinley had some protection, but lax security allowed his assassin to carry a gun right up to where he could shoot point-blank at the president [64].

On 14 September 1901 Theodore Roosevelt was sworn in as the twenty-sixth President of the United States. Roosevelt was one of the two most important national figures of the Progressive Era. Along with Woodrow Wilson he came to represent the age of reform. Roosevelt remains one of the most well-known and celebrated American presidents. His distinctive smile, pince-nez glasses, and Rough Rider hat make him instantly recognizable. Even though he hated the nickname 'Teddy' and no one who knew him well ever called him by it, he became 'Teddy' for the American people during his years in office. The youngest man ever to hold the office of president, he imparted a spirit of youthful energy and ebullience to everything he did. The presidency, he said, was a 'bully pulpit' and he preached the lessons of duty and national responsibility to his fellow citizens [65 p. 10].

Although he was a man of the people, Roosevelt came from an upper-class background. Born in 1858 in New York City to wealthy parents, Roosevelt was a sickly youth who suffered from asthma and allergies. Inspired by his father, he worked hard to build up his body and by the time he graduated from Harvard College in 1880 he had become a strong physical specimen. Unlike many aristocratic young men of his class, he then plunged into politics, and was elected to the New York State Assembly in 1881. During the next three years he received a thorough education in the rough-and-tumble politics of the nation's largest state. Reporters followed eagerly the activities of Roosevelt, who seemed to attract publicity wherever he went [65].

In 1884 personal tragedy struck. His young wife died giving birth to a daughter and Roosevelt's mother died the same day. Seeking solace for these personal losses, Roosevelt went west to his cattle ranch in Dakota Territory where he worked cattle and lived in the open. While he lost money in the ranching business, he gained valuable western connections that contributed to his national appeal. In 1886 he married a childhood friend named Edith Carow and began the large family that would make the White House such a boisterous place during his presidency.

Roosevelt was also getting back into politics. He ran unsuccessfully for mayor of New York City in 1886, and then served on the United States Civil Service Commission under Presidents Benjamin Harrison and Grover Cleveland. He left that post in 1895 after six years in Washington to become a member of the New York City Police Commission. When the Republicans regained the presidency in 1896, Roosevelt lobbied hard to be named Assistant Secretary of the Navy in 1897. Back in Washington he became a strong voice for naval preparedness and war with Spain.

When the two nations went to war in April 1898, Roosevelt helped raise a regiment of volunteers to go to Cuba. Roosevelt's father had not served in the Civil War, and his son was determined not to miss his own chance at combat and personal redemption. Even his wife's serious illness did not deter him from volunteering. In Cuba, Roosevelt's heroic performance with his unit, which reporters named 'The Rough Riders,' made him an American hero. That in turn led to his nomination for governor in New York a few months later. The presidency, which he so much wanted, came to him when McKinley was killed. As he told his close friend, Senator

Henry Cabot Lodge of Massachusetts, 'it is a dreadful thing to come to the presidency in this way, but it would be a far worse thing to be morbid about it' [65 p. 2].

In office, Roosevelt brought excitement and a rare sense of fun to the conduct of the presidency. His family made excellent copy for the newspapers. His young sons, who became 'The White House Gang,' captivated the public with their antics. On one occasion, the youngest boy, Quentin, used the White House elevator to bring his sick brother Archie his 350-pound calico pony. His oldest daughter, Alice, from his first marriage, emerged as a national celebrity. She was known as 'Princess Alice,' who had a pet snake called 'Emily Spinach' and smoked in public. Newspapers reported that she might be married to one of the royal princes of Europe. As Alice raced around Washington in an automobile and enjoyed a brisk social life, her father was reported to have told a friend, 'I can be President of the United States, or I can attend to Alice. I can't do both' [65 p. 104].

Roosevelt's energy and ebullience made the White House a center of news and a focus of attention. The president invited guests to the White House across the whole spectrum of American society from poets to athletes, and he imparted the sense that governing was an activity that was challenging and worthwhile. As a result, he drew young men into government and infused the bureaucracy with his own energy and drive. In his autobiography, Roosevelt proudly quoted the remarks of an English writer in 1908 who said that the president had 'gathered around him a body of public servants who are nowhere surpassed, I question whether they are anywhere equaled, for efficiency, self-sacrifice, and an absolute devotion to their country's interests' [65 p. 197].

Roosevelt approached the presidency with personal drive and a desire to make his administration notable in American history. He devised what came to be known as the 'stewardship' theory of the office. The president, he maintained, was the steward of the American people and, as the chief executive, should try to do the things that his fellow citizens wanted accomplished. If the Constitution did not expressly prohibit the president from doing some course of action, then the occupant of the White House had a duty to use his power for the benefit of the people. In Roosevelt's mind that meant creating national parks, exercising strong leadership in foreign policy, and attacking the corrupt influence of corporate monopoly and bigness. His pursuit of these worthy goals sometimes led Roosevelt to stretch or bend the Constitution.

At the same time, Roosevelt was a pragmatic politician who knew that he could not do more than the Republican party in Congress would allow him to accomplish. When he took office in September 1901 the Grand Old Party had large majorities in both houses of Congress. The leadership of the Republicans, particularly in the United States Senate, was very conservative.

Roosevelt realized that he could not confront those leaders directly without endangering his presidency. As a result, his first priority was to win election in his own right in 1904. While he was careful not to alienate the congressional leaders between 1901 and 1904, he also moved ahead to put his own stamp on the presidency.

In doing so, Roosevelt delivered a powerful stimulus to the emerging reform movement. He demonstrated that vigorous presidential leadership could frame issues and set priorities. He raised questions such as the conservation of natural resources, the proper way to manage the power of large corporations, and the balance between labor and capital. His example also encouraged younger politicians to enter government service and to embark on reform careers.

Roosevelt's first dramatic move in his effort to reshape the nation's priorities occurred in February 1902 when he instructed the Justice Department to file an antitrust suit against the Northern Securities Company, the railroad combination that James J. Hill, E.H. Harriman, and J.P. Morgan had assembled in late 1901. The Sherman Antitrust Act had not been used much as a weapon against the trusts in the Cleveland and McKinley administrations. The Supreme Court, in the case of *US* v. *E.C. Knight* (1895), had rendered a decision that had left the act much less effective. The Court had said that the government could not break up the Sugar Trust merely because it had a monopoly of manufacturing sugar in the United States. There had to be what the Court called a monopoly of commerce to warrant antitrust action. Roosevelt intended to challenge the Court's ruling and see if the Sherman Act could be revitalized. He believed that 'the Nation should, without interfering with the power of the States in the matter itself, also assume power of supervision and regulation over all corporations doing an interstate business' [65 p. 33].

Roosevelt's action sent a shock through Wall Street. When he learned that the Justice Department had filed the suit, J.P. Morgan hurried to the White House to see if further lawsuits were planned. Roosevelt assured him that they were not, as long as the companies conducted themselves in a responsible manner. The case itself went through the courts until it culminated in a narrow decision for the government in 1904. The Northern Securities Company was dissolved. Roosevelt noted proudly of the 1895 E.C. Knight case: 'This decision I caused to be annulled by the court that had rendered it' [72; 65 p. 49].

Beyond the specifics of the case, Roosevelt's actions showed to the American people that the president shared their concern about the role of big business in the nation's life. Roosevelt gained a reputation as a trust-buster that he never lost. His fame was a little misleading. Roosevelt was not an opponent of bigness in business in and of itself. He was evolving the distinction that he would develop between socially useful businesses (good trusts) and corporate predators or outlaws (bad trusts). Before he could address that problem, however, he thought that it was imperative to establish the government's supremacy over any single corporation. He called large corporations 'the creatures of the State,' and contended that 'the State not only has the right to control them, but it is in duty bound to control them wherever the need of such control is shown' [28 *p. 35*].

THE SQUARE DEAL

Later in 1902 Roosevelt launched a second presidential campaign that gained wide popular approval. In the spring of that year the United Mine Workers union walked off the job in the anthracite (hard coal) mines of Pennsylvania. The strike ran for months, and as fall approached the possibility of coal shortages for the winter months loomed. In a time before the widespread use of oil or natural gas, coal was the main reliance of Americans for heat in the winter. Republicans also worried that a continuation of the walkout might threaten their control of Congress in the fall elections. If the strike went on the party in power would be blamed for the hardships that average Americans would encounter.

Roosevelt decided that it was the president's duty to intervene to end the crisis. Although there was no direct precedent for government intervention in a labor dispute, Roosevelt believed that the public interest warranted vigorous executive action. Accordingly, he summoned the coal mine operators and the union leaders to the White House for a conference in early October 1902. This was a gesture of large historical significance for Roosevelt's presidency and the development of reform. Eight years earlier, during the Pullman Strike of 1894, President Grover Cleveland had sent in the army to break the strikes and had sought legal injunctions against the unions involved. Now Roosevelt was placing capital and labor on an equal footing. It was the kind of public gesture that Roosevelt was beginning to call 'The Square Deal' [24; 72]. The unions proved receptive to presidential action; the coal men and their railroad allies rejected Roosevelt's intervention.

Roosevelt went even further. When the deadlock between the two parties persisted, he explored ways in which the federal government might use the armed forces to operate the mines. That threat and the pressure of the elections persuaded the mine owners to agree to a settlement. A commission was named to arbitrate the dispute. It gave the miners a pay increase, but not the official recognition that the union sought. Nonetheless, Roosevelt had averted a domestic crisis and had clearly tilted toward the workers in this battle with management. The coal strike intervention became a model for future executive policies when labor unrest occurred. It also added what one writer called 'the color of romance and knight errantry' to the 'prosaic office' of the presidency and 'heightened the appeal' of Roosevelt's character [65 *p. 71*].

The president's commitment to social reform was a cautious one. A conservative man at heart, he wanted to provide gradual change to stave off more sweeping alterations in the nation's social order. He saw the presidency as a bulwark against Socialism and disorder. He advised his fellow Republicans that a posture of unyielding resistance to popular clamor was dangerous. It was necessary, Roosevelt argued, 'to make big man and little man alike obey the law' [28 *p. 34*].

In one sensitive area, however, Roosevelt was careful not to disturb the feelings of white Americans. By the early years of the twentieth century, racial segregation had become an accepted fact of life in the South. For many white southerners, the 'progressive' answer to their social problems was to rid their politics of what they believed was the corrupting impact of black voters. The years of Roosevelt's presidency represented one of the low periods of race relations in the United States. Lynchings were common in the South, and members of the Democratic party in Congress proposed the repeal of the Fourteenth and Fifteenth Amendments that had been passed during the Reconstruction Era. There were no longer any black members of Congress, and the majority of African Americans in the South were barred from the political process. In a state such as Texas, laws were adopted to make sure that black citizens could not take part in the deliberations of the Democratic party that dominated public life. As a Democratic leader in the state put it, 'in the absence of universal intelligence the only safeguard for a permanent democracy will be found in restricting suffrage to those who in *some way* show an honest interest in public affairs' [*Doc. 10*; 33; 77].

For Roosevelt this meant that the Republican party in the South was largely an all-black organization devoted to maximizing its influence at the time of the presidential nominating conventions and securing as much federal patronage as possible. That explained why, in the early months of his presidency, he had the black leader Booker T. Washington to the White House as his dinner guest. When the news came out, the South erupted with charges that the president was pursuing social equality between blacks and whites. A Memphis editor wrote that the dinner was 'the most damnable outrage that has ever been perpetrated by any citizen of the United States.' Roosevelt's real aim was nothing of the sort. He wanted to gain Washington's influence to help him control the Republican nomination in 1904 [65 *p. 23*].

In pursuing this course, Roosevelt was recognizing the power of racism in early twentieth-century America. A presidential crusade on behalf of racial justice would have been doomed to embarrassing failure. Sharing many of the prejudices of his fellow white citizens, Roosevelt made few gestures on behalf of a more equitable society. For most whites, progressive and conservative, the status of black people in the United States seemed to be off the agenda of reform throughout most of the Progressive Era. This attitude would continue in the presidencies of William Howard Taft and Woodrow Wilson. Blacks themselves and a few white supporters would provide the energy for changing the racial situation of the United States later in the decade.

After an initial flurry of presidential activism in 1901–2, Roosevelt slowed down his program in 1903–4 to insure that his nomination by the Republicans would be uncontested. He did achieve results in foreign policy that assisted his presidential candidacy. The most controversial of these actions came in Panama, where Roosevelt tacitly encouraged a revolt of the people of that area against their rulers in Colombia. When the uprising occurred, American war vessels were offshore. The treaty with the new Panamanian government giving the United States the right to construct a canal and a zone through which to do it was heavily weighted in favor of Washington. Roosevelt was acting out his favorite adage as a diplomat: 'Speak softly and carry a big stick' [24 *pp. 50–1*].

Divided and in disarray, the Democratic party decided not to try to run to the left of the popular president. Weary of the two defeats at the hands of William Jennings Bryan in 1896 and 1900, the Democrats elected to try to attack Roosevelt as a potential dictator who was not conservative enough. In 1903 and 1904, the party rallied behind an obscure New York state judge named Alton B. Parker, who had the virtues of having asserted few controversial opinions on any topic for the preceding decade. If Parker could carry New York State against Roosevelt, that accomplishment along with the solidly Democratic base in the South might give the opposition an outside chance at an upset in 1904.

As a result, the election in 1904 matched the colorless Parker against the ebullient Roosevelt. Parker, said one unfriendly newspaper, had 'all the salient qualities of a sphere.' By trying to seem more safe and sane than Roosevelt, the Democrats insured that the election would turn on the president's attractive personal qualities. That meant a certain victory for Theodore Roosevelt. In keeping with the custom that an incumbent president should not openly seek votes, Roosevelt stayed off the campaign trail and allowed other Republicans to make the case for another four years in office. The campaign was dull until the last few days when Parker attacked Roosevelt as an agent of the big corporations. While it was true that the Republicans had accepted campaign contributions from big business, the notion that Theodore Roosevelt was the docile instrument of Wall Street was a tough sell to voters in 1904. The president won a smashing election victory in which he received 336 electoral votes to 140 for Parker. It was the highest number of electoral votes any presidential candidate had received up to that time. As one newspaper observed, the American people regarded the president as 'the most popular man that has come into public life within recent times' [28 *p. 57; 65 p. 145*].

On election night, Theodore Roosevelt announced that he would not be a candidate for another term as president in 1908. He did so to deflect Democratic charges that he would stay in office for life. The declaration helped to shape the course of American politics for the decade that followed in ways that Roosevelt had not anticipated when he made it. In time it would prove to have been one of his worst mistakes. In November 1904, however, it seemed to Theodore Roosevelt that he had established himself as president in his own right and could now turn to enacting the policy reforms that he believed were necessary. During the early months of 1905, the outlines of progressive politics in the United States began to take shape.

CHAPTER THREE

THE RISING TIDE OF PROGRESSIVE REFORM

In the years that followed Theodore Roosevelt's election in 1904, the spirit of progressive reform became a dominant element in American public life. A number of causes came together in 1905 and 1906 to inspire advocates of change with the possibility of redirecting society. Theodore Roosevelt played a large role in this process, but progressivism extended well beyond Washington and the White House.

The economic prosperity that had begun during the last years of the 1890s was now a happy fact of national life. Wages were rising, though not as fast as prices, and employment stood at high levels. The hard times of the 1890s were a fading memory. As a result, Americans now thought of themselves as consumers of the bounties of an industrial society as much as producers of its goods and services. Middle-class citizens paid more attention when their daily newspapers told them that the patent medicines they took for illnesses and the foods they ate each day might be unsafe or even deadly. Sentiment arose for government to take action to safeguard consumers against dangerous products.

The problems of child labor and alcohol also gained renewed attention during the middle of the decade. The movement of textile mills from North to South in pursuit of cheaper labor costs focused reformers on the plight of the thousands of children under sixteen who worked twelve hours a day, six days a week, at their machines. They were, said the Michigan State Federation of Women's Clubs, 'toiling under the glorious flag of liberty to satisfy the greed of commercialism' [Doc. 11].

The lobbying efforts of the Anti-Saloon League linked the traffic in alcohol to other reform issues. For the advocates of liquor restriction, the saloon corrupted politics, broke up families, and caused industrial accidents. Where the power of evangelical Christians was strong in the South and West, the crusade against alcohol became a key to progressivism after 1905. One academic writer of the day, John Marshall Barker, argued 'for a strenuous and vehement crusade against the saloon as the enemy of social well-being and progress' [Doc. 7].

With a bright future ahead for the United States and the prospect of enduring domestic and international peace, reformers believed that a modest amount of government intervention into the economy could adjust the inequities of society without disturbing the fundamental balance of a free economy. Since human nature was essentially good and could be improved, government should endeavor to encourage citizens to behave in a socially rewarding manner. At a time when the size of the state and national government was modest, a small increase in size did not seem likely to produce an all-powerful state [29 *pp. 35–40*].

THE PROGRESSIVE AGENDA

Implementing these goals that most progressives shared produced two contrasting approaches to reform. Many progressives contended that the answer to the problems of democracy was even more democracy: that is, to make government and its operations more accessible to the people and less the plaything of party politicians. The party system with its backroom deals and rigged conventions seemed an obstacle to such changes because of its control of how candidates were nominated and elected. The dominance that the parties exerted in Congress and state legislatures, and the inability of average citizens to express their displeasure with corrupt or inefficient public officials, seemed less and less appropriate for a modern society [35].

As a result, the reform movement devised a number of procedural changes that aimed at opening up the political process to influences from outside the smoke-filled rooms of the state machines or the powerful lobbyist. One favorite answer was the direct primary. This method allowed voters to select candidates of their political party in an election rather than a caucus or convention. A reformer such as Robert M. La Follette of Wisconsin used the direct primary issue to his advantage in the late 1890s as he battled the Republican leaders on the road to the governorship. Once in office after 1901, La Follette made the primary one of the key parts of his program for reform in Wisconsin. His reliance on that procedural change led to a bitter battle within the Wisconsin Republican party that dominated the state's politics for years [24; 58; 59].

A related change was a proposed amendment to the Constitution to have United States senators also elected by the voters themselves. Up to that time, the selection was made by the individual state legislatures, where, it was charged, corrupt and backstage forces often dictated the choice of millionaires or individuals loyal to the party bosses. Allowing the voters to make the senatorial designation might reduce the power of rich men in the Senate and find individuals more responsive to the needs of the average American. Meanwhile, journalists wrote articles exposing the Senate as the 'rich man's club' and saying that the upper house was guilty of 'treason' for the way it mishandled the interests of the people. Such rich lawmakers as Chauncey Depew of New York, Nelson Aldrich of Rhode Island, and John F. Dryden of New Jersey came to symbolize the presence of wealth in the upper house of Congress [24; 35].

On the scale of progressive innovation, the referendum seemed an even more radical and sweeping step. It proposed that the electorate should be asked for its opinion on controversial issues, rather than leaving those matters to be resolved by a corruptible legislature. So if the prohibition of alcohol, for example, was a burning question for the voters of Texas or Mississippi, then they should have the right to indicate by their votes what they wanted their elected representatives to do about it [28; 35].

Some reformers went even further. Men such as William S. U'Ren of Oregon contended that voters should even have the authority to propose laws themselves. That became known as the 'initiative' in which enough voters might gather signatures for a petition drive to have a law adopted or a referendum called. Finally, and sometimes most controversial of all, was the 'recall'. This idea said that if a public official, such as a judge or mayor, had become corrupt or out-of-touch with public opinion, the voters might ask for an election at which the ouster of the office-holder could be decided. If the vote ran against the incumbent, then he would be 'recalled' from office and a vacancy produced. An election to fill the place would follow [35].

In the minds of conservatives, none of these procedural changes had much appeal. They all involved a greater degree of popular participation in the political process than seemed wise or appropriate. The most dangerous one was the recall. Believing that an independent judiciary stood against the winds of popular opinion, conservatives thought that the ability to oust a judge for a controversial decision would undermine respect for the law. Critics of the judiciary countered that undemocratic rulings by unelected judges against the popular opinion of the time represented an equally dangerous threat to the workings of the political system.

Despite conservative objections, a number of states had adopted one or more of these new approaches by 1905. South Dakota led the way with the initiative and referendum in 1908 and some twenty states introduced these techniques in the years that followed. The recall appeared first in the Los Angeles city charter in 1903, and voters used it to remove a city councilman in 1904. Oregon was the first state to use the procedure. Ten others followed suit [35].

All of these measures reflected a deep suspicion of the political party that pervaded progressivism. The popular magazine *The Saturday Evening Post* observed in 1905 that 'the people have come to see that parties are to a great extent the tools of the unscrupulous men who make of politics a profession.' Progressives asserted that government should not be run on a partisan basis. After all, there was no Democratic or Republican method of fighting fires, cleaning streets, or managing utilities. Leading thinkers of the time, heavily influenced by the experience of attending colleges and universities, came to see politics as an unsavory, inherently corrupt enterprise that rarely produced good results for society [28 *p. 35*].

The devices of partisanship also grew to seem old hat and out of date. The rallies, lengthy speeches, and protracted campaigns of the 1880s and 1890s were deemed relics of the past. 'The people,' said one news account in 1900, 'have grown tired of the same campaign speeches, a repetition of bonfires, noise of the anvil and fireworks and all that went to awaken enthusiasm.' What the voters needed, the progressive argued, was a form of elections that stressed issues, not emotions, an appeal to reason rather than to the heart of a partisan [36 *pp. 146–7*].

As a result, campaigns during the Progressive Era became more oriented toward advertising and merchandising techniques. The marketing of candidates with films and billboards was a profession that anticipated the modern use of consultants. In the process, campaigns also found their costs rising as the parties had to reach voters individually rather than through a collective experience such as a rally or a march. Rising costs meant an increased dependence on corporate contributions to pay for an election campaign [36].

THE RISE OF REGULATION

The same suspicion of partisanship underlay a complementary trend of progressivism toward the use of experts rather than politicians in making public policy decisions. At a time when institutions in American society were becoming more professionalized, there was a logic to the argument that trained individuals could make better informed decisions about technical issues of railroad regulation, city design, or social justice than an elected representative beholden to special interests with no special competence or technical expertise [35].

The favored procedure for implementing government supervision of this kind was the regulatory agency, but other boards and commissions also appeared during the first years of the century to carry out the policies of the state for overseeing road building, conservation programs, and supervision of professions. The loser in this process was the political party, which found its ability to place partisans in government jobs reduced and its capacity to affect policy diminished. The claims of efficiency and economy meant a curtailed role for the traditional political organizations [35; 44].

Some good came of these changes. Political appointees had often been more noteworthy for their connections than their competence. The more notorious forms of corruption lessened as clear rules and practices replaced informal networks of friends and loose understandings. Organized, precise budgets replaced older spending techniques. Academically informed experts carried their knowledge from the classroom to the state house. The most notable example of this trend came in Wisconsin where Governor Robert M. La Follette tapped the brainpower at the University of Wisconsin to write legislation, serve on commissions, and advise him on policy alternatives. This intimate relationship between politicians and professors became known as 'The Wisconsin Idea' [26].

Reliance on experts was a natural development as society became more organized and interdependent, but it had anti-democratic implications that not all progressives grasped at the time. The rough-and-tumble of partisan politics meant that an official was accountable to the voters even in the most one-party states. An expert appointee, insulated from partisan considerations, could make decisions that affected the citizens of a state or city without fear of direct electoral reprisal. In addition, the reforms assumed that all or most of the experts would arrive at progressive decisions. But everything hinged on who did the appointing. When conservatives came into office, they were able to put their choices onto boards and commissions, and then the experts could make judgments that belied the hopes of the progressives who had created the agency or commission. The transition to expert regulation was on the whole a wise and proper development, but it was not the universal answer to the problems of an industrial society that some progressives envisioned [35; 92].

ROOSEVELT'S REGULATORY CAMPAIGN

An important step toward this form of regulation on the national level occurred in 1905–6 when Theodore Roosevelt pressed a campaign to control railroads through strengthening the Interstate Commerce Commission (ICC). Founded in 1887, the Commission had seen its authority over rates and railroad practices diminished through adverse court rulings in the 1890s. Meanwhile, shippers and other railroad customers filed complaints about the conduct of rail lines in giving rebates (discounts on published rates) to favored users of railroads or discriminating in favor of one locality over another [24; 28; 44].

In 1903–4, pressure for remedial legislation mounted as midwestern politicians and their constituents urged Congress to act. Following his election in 1904, Roosevelt took up the regulatory cause in his annual (State of the Union) message. 'The government must in increasing degree supervise and regulate the workings of the railways engaged in interstate commerce,' the president asserted. Roosevelt had found a cause that pleased the public as much as his earlier attacks on the trusts. The railroads occupied a place in American life at the beginning of the twentieth century that made them an economic necessity to the nation. Since their services affected so many people, they became the focus for economic discontent much as would large oil companies at the end of the century. Popular fears about the impact of business consolidation centered on the activities of the railroads. As worries about rising consumer prices intensified, the railroads were seen as a major element in inflationary pressures [65 *p. 149*; 81; 82].

In pursuing railroad regulation from late 1904 through mid-1906, Roosevelt wielded presidential power in a manner that would become characteristic of strong executives for the rest of the century. He worked with Congress to shape the form of the legislation itself, he went out on speaking tours on behalf of his railroad program, and he used other instruments of the federal government to insure that his proposals received favorable action. The Justice Department filed anti-rebating cases that illustrated railroad misdeeds. During the winter and spring of 1905, Roosevelt told audiences around the country of the need for greater power for the ICC. He remarked to the Union League Club of Philadelphia on 30 January that Americans would not 'permanently tolerate the use of vast power conferred by vast wealth' without giving the federal government the 'still higher power of seeing that this power in addition to being used in the interest of individual or individuals possessing it, is also used for and not against the interest of the people as a whole' [65 *p. 152*; *Docs 8 and 9*].

RISING PUBLIC SUPPORT FOR REFORM

Roosevelt's language set the stage for a battle over railroad regulation that went on for the next two years. It also reflected the president's shrewd grasp of the attitudes and feelings of the American people. By the spring of 1905 the sentiment for reform of the political system was gathering momentum. Americans were reading in their popular magazines about the extent to which business interests had influenced politics to their advantage. In June 1905 a New York clergyman told an Iowa senator, 'The whole country is keenly sensitive to the perils of corporate wealth and the decline of the great convictions' [28 *p. 75*].

A series of scandals erupted across the country. In Texas, Senator Joseph Weldon Bailey came under fire for an alleged corrupt involvement with a subsidiary of Standard Oil. California and Pennsylvania voters witnessed spectacular graft trials in which public officials were charged with taking bribes. The issue of railroad domination became central in southern and western states. A few months after Roosevelt's election the nation was in the midst of a political storm. 'There is a craze on now not at all unlike what preceded the Alliance and Populist movement,' said a Kansas Republican in the late winter of 1905 [29 *pp. 67–8*; 35].

The most dramatic revelations occurred when the internal workings of gas and insurance companies came under scrutiny in New York State. A young lawyer named Charles Evans Hughes was chosen to make the probe, and his relentless digging uncovered examples of bribes and huge campaign contributions that shocked middle-class voters. The interrelationships among these large corporations and the political parties seemed especially sinister. As one reporter recalled, 'a large number of thoughtful Americans were growing increasingly anxious or indignant about the lawless conditions existing in so many walks of our life' [*4 p. 161*].

The journalists who had begun to expose corporate abuses in popular periodicals a few years earlier were now at the peak of their influence. In addition to Lincoln Steffens and Ida Tarbell, Ray Stannard Baker had been instrumental in arousing anger against railroad abuses. Samuel Hopkins Adams was looking into the patent medicine industry where extravagant medical claims and shoddy products dominated the scene. Each month Americans picked up their favorite magazine and learned of how senators were in the pockets of large corporations, how state legislators were corruptly influenced, and how laws were bent or broken to avoid a public outcry. The major publications, *Collier's, The World's Work,* and *American Magazine,* vied with each other to expose the next example of corporate or political misdeeds [7; 13; 31].

ROOSEVELT'S REGULATORY PROGRAM

This atmosphere of exposure helped Theodore Roosevelt's campaign for railroad regulation during the winter and spring of 1906. Getting a regulatory bill through the House of Representatives presented few problems. The forces of reform were strong, especially within the Democratic party, and the conservative Republicans could cast a politically safe vote for regulation knowing that the Senate would be less cordial to the president. The House adopted a regulatory measure named after William P. Hepburn of Iowa, and national attention shifted to the Senate. Seasoned political observers predicted that the Senate Republican leader, Nelson Aldrich of Rhode Island, would amend the House version to make it more suitable to conservative opinion. In the Senate since 1881, Aldrich saw little merit in regulation, but knew that some sort of law was likely to pass [*Doc. 9*; 65].

A pitched parliamentary battle ensued in which Aldrich used all of the legislative devices he could muster to water down the president's bill. After three months, both sides claimed victory in what became known as the Hepburn Act of 1906. The advantage lay with the White House. Roosevelt had achieved much of what he had sought. The Interstate Commerce Commission gained more authority over rates and the power to scrutinize the books of the railroad companies. Roosevelt believed that he had accomplished a great deal against determined opposition. Progressives agreed that if it had not been for Roosevelt's presidential leadership, no bill would have come out of the Senate at all [24].

The congressional session took action on other regulatory measures. The work of crusading journalists such as Samuel Hopkins Adams had alerted Americans to problems with the foods that they ate and the patent medicines they used to treat a variety of ills. The popular uproar that ensued led to a pure food and drugs bill that was stuck in Congress during the spring of 1906 [24; 25].

The publication of a sensational novel by a Socialist writer, Upton Sinclair, galvanized public opinion on a topic even more closely connected to the everyday concerns of Americans than patent medicine. In his book *The Jungle*, Sinclair offered a vivid and often sickening description of how the meat-packing industry operated in the Chicago stockyards. Written to convert Americans to Socialism, the book did not have that result, but it did nauseate middle-class readers. Sinclair quipped that he had aimed at the hearts of the American people and instead had hit them in the stomach [25].

The outrage that accompanied Sinclair's book stirred Congress to adopt an amendment to the Agriculture Appropriation bill calling for federal inspection of the meat-packing business. Roosevelt threw his support behind the law and worked with friendly senators to see it enacted. The furor over meat-packing also helped the pure food and drug bill emerge from the House and it too was enacted in late June 1906. In what had become a highly productive session, Roosevelt had accomplished what he termed 'a noteworthy advance in the policy of securing Federal supervision and control over corporations' [65 p. 169].

ROOSEVELT AND THE MUCKRAKERS

In the process of working to enact these bills, however, Roosevelt also undercut the reporters who had been so instrumental in arousing public opinion for reform. The exposés had begun to touch on the leaders of the Republican party in Congress who enjoyed such close financial ties to the business community. The intensity with which men such as Lincoln Steffens and Ray Stannard Baker went after their business targets worried the president, who did not wish to see reform go too far. Roosevelt warned the journalists to temper their criticism of the Senate and corporations. In April 1906 he delivered a speech in which he compared these reporters to a character in John Milton's *Pilgrim's Progress* who spent so much time raking the muck on the floor that he failed to see heaven above him. The reporters became known as 'muckrakers,' and that label came to stand for all the journalists who specialized in uncovering graft and corruption [*Doc. 12*; 5; 7; 24].

The presidential slap that Roosevelt delivered to the muckrakers came at a time when popular interest in their product was beginning to wane. Publishers found that happier and more optimistic articles, and even light fiction, attracted a wider readership. The fashion for muckraking slowed and then stopped. Some traces of the craft remained during the years before World War I, but the heyday of that kind of journalism was over. [31].

Despite this trend, the muckrakers had made a significant contribution to the reform process. Without their aggressive reporting, many of the problems of the period would not have come to public notice in as dramatic a fashion. Reporters such as Tarbell, Steffens, Baker, and Adams were better at pointing out problems than developing solutions, but their role in identifying issues was crucial. Their legacy was a permanent one in American journalism.

THE 1906 ELECTIONS

The work of Congress in the first half of 1906 set the stage for the next dramatic phase of reform during the congressional elections of that year. The American labor movement, recovering from the difficulties of the 1890s, decided to throw its weight into the races for Congress. Samuel Gompers and the American Federation of Labor (AFL) issued 'Labor's Bill of Rights' and petitioned lawmakers to implement their program. They asked the Republicans and Democrats to support what labor wanted. When the Republicans predictably declined to do so, the AFL threw in its lot with the Democrats. In their campaign literature, the Democrats responded that their party was 'First to Recognize Organized Labor.' This development foreshadowed future links between Democrats and organized labor [28; 43 *p. 22*].

Another element in the 1906 election was the Socialist party led by Eugene Victor Debs and the Industrial Workers of the World (IWW), known as the 'Wobblies.' The IWW had split off from the other Socialists in 1905 and thought that the American Federation of Labor was too conservative to achieve real social change. Debs caught that spirit when he said, 'The choice is between the A.F. of L. and capitalism on the one side and the industrial workers and socialism on the other.' Internal feuding and disputes about which direction to take limited the effectiveness of the Wobblies in 1906–7, but they offered an inviting target for conservatives eager to discredit the labor movement [27 *p. 107*; 70].

Theodore Roosevelt and other progressive reformers did not admire the Socialists and their ideas. Government ownership of business went too far. One of the key elements in the president's decision to pursue economic and political reform was the fear that if he did not act, more radical policies would become popular. 'There are great numbers of radicals who think we have not gone far enough,' said Roosevelt in August 1906, 'and a great number of reactionaries who think we have gone altogether too far and we array against ourselves both the sordid beneficiaries of the evils we assail and the wild-eyed agitators who tend to indiscriminate assault on everything good and bad alike.' In 1906, however, this position meant for Roosevelt a vigorous attack on the IWW and the AFL as being too sweeping in their attacks on the administration, the Republicans, and Roosevelt's policies [3 *vol. V, p. 366*].

For Roosevelt, then, progressivism as he conceived it did not involve an assault on capitalism and private property. Instead it looked to the wise use of governmental power to make constructive changes and thus forestall more radical answers. This position has led scholars to claim that Roosevelt was fundamentally a conservative figure. If that means that he did not embrace Marxist solutions to the problems of early twentieth-century America, then the charge is a valid one, if somewhat irrelevant to the realities of American politics. If this argument contends that Roosevelt saw no difference between himself and the more conservative, not to say reactionary, leaders of his party, then it is a misreading of the political context of Roosevelt's actions.

There was a strong strain of conservative suspicion of increased government regulation within the Republican party by 1906. The older willingness to use an activist national government to stimulate the economy was giving way to a dislike of the use of federal power to adjust economic and social arrangements against wealth and privilege. Where they had long scoffed at Democratic contentions about the value of state rights, now Republicans were finding renewed worth in the idea that the national government should be limited in its powers and influence on the economy. To the extent that progressivism implied a larger role for the federal government in the workings of politics and public policy, many Republicans by 1906 were deciding that they were not in fact progressives at all.

The Democrats for their part were experiencing similar internal disagreements about where they should stand on the issue of regulation. A government powerful enough to supervise corporations and regulate railroads might also be strong enough to tell southern states that black Americans could vote. The race issue remained a strong check on the willingness of Democrats to take advantage of Republican disunity and become the party of broadened national power. However, some leading Democrats, such as William Jennings Bryan, while being careful not to alienate the South over race, came out for government control of the railroads in 1906. The two parties were evolving toward the positions they would adopt on government regulation for the next century [43; 67].

The 1906 elections did not resolve these emerging tensions about government regulation within both of the major parties. If anything the results suggested that the issue would remain a source of contention for each party well into the future. The Democrats did not make the dramatic gains in the House of Representatives that they had hoped to see when the year began. They reduced the Republican majority down from 112 seats to 55, but made only marginal gains elsewhere. Theodore Roosevelt's strong endorsement of the Republican Congress and the vigorous campaign of his surrogates against labor radicalism slowed Democratic progress. Yet, the opposition party had built an electoral base from which it would expand during the next three election cycles, culminating in the election of Woodrow Wilson to the presidency in 1912 [43].

For the moment, the Republicans felt the impact of the dispute most directly. With Roosevelt's term entering its last two years, his conservative enemies in Congress felt freer to oppose his regulatory policies. Speaker Joseph G. Cannon of the House of Representatives led the opposition to Roosevelt's call for inheritance taxes, income taxes, and tighter supervision of corporations. Such measures rarely received consideration in the lower house in 1906–7. An Illinois representative renowned for his crude language, Cannon was so conservative that it was said in Washington that had he been present when the universe was created, he would have voted for chaos [28].

The lawmakers also felt emboldened to attack Roosevelt in one of his favorite areas of national policy. Since taking office, Roosevelt had spoken to his fellow citizens about the need to conserve the nation's natural resources. 'The forest and water problems,' he said in 1901, 'are perhaps the most vital internal questions of the United States.' He used his executive powers to establish bird refuges, create national parks, and set aside endangered areas from development. All of these actions he justified as a wise use of presidential authority [10; 65 *p. 41*].

The main agent for carrying out Roosevelt's conservation aims was the Chief Forester, Gifford Pinchot. One of the few trained conservationists in the government, the aristocratic Pinchot believed that natural resources should be set aside for future wise and prudent use in the economy. He did not like reckless development, but neither was he a believer in preservation of wilderness areas for their own sake. In this stance, Pinchot and Roosevelt had similar views. They saw the federal government as exercising prudent control in the national interest rather than allowing people in the states and regions to go forward in a careless and unplanned way. They believed in applying expertise to the use of natural resources much as other progressives were committed to informed regulation in handling railroads, corporate behavior, and social justice [10].

Roosevelt's conservation policies created controversy. Larger corporations endorsed the programs because they provided certainty about what governments might do and what would be expected of businesses.

Advocates of conservation applauded the impulse to manage resources carefully. Some members of the emerging conservation coalition distrusted Pinchot and Roosevelt's readiness to introduce government bureaucrats and corporate power into the wild places of the United States. The most strident opposition to what the president and his aide were doing came from westerners themselves who did not want decisions about what was logged, mined, or farmed to be made in Washington [79; 83].

That western unhappiness with Roosevelt surfaced during the session of Congress that met after the 1906 elections. With adjournment mandated for 4 March 1907, lawmakers introduced language in an appropriation bill to bar 'except by act of Congress' the creation of new forest reserves in six states in the West. Knowing that he could not veto an appropriation bill at that last minute, Roosevelt worked quickly with Pinchot to issue proclamations creating forest reserves in the affected states before the new law went into effect. Western discontent with Roosevelt and conservation would reappear in an important controversy of the Taft administration [65 *p. 203*].

THE BROWNSVILLE RAID AND RACE RELATIONS

In the aftermath of the 1906 election, another controversy involving Roosevelt illustrated the continuing problem of race relations within Progressive Era America. In August 1906 a shooting incident had occurred in Brownsville, Texas, for which black soldiers at a nearby fort were blamed. White townspeople complained that blacks had been engaged in random shooting. The evidence against the men was very weak, and the most logical explanation was that townspeople had staged the episode to have the African-American soldiers removed. Nonetheless, the army and Theodore Roosevelt believed that the black troops were guilty, especially when they denied all knowledge of what had taken place. The president instinctively believed that whites told the truth and African Americans did not [76].

The day after the congressional elections, Roosevelt discharged all three companies of African-American soldiers without a hearing and without a trial. The ensuing uproar led to congressional hearings. Throughout all of the proceedings that followed, Roosevelt steadfastly declined to admit that he might have made a mistake or been hasty in his judgment. The president became entangled in a bitter dispute with the main senatorial defender of the men, Joseph B. Foraker, of Ohio. Despite the efforts of Foraker and other champions of the soldiers, they did not receive justice from the army or the president [76].

It was not a good time for black Americans. In 1908 whites rioted against blacks in Springfield, Illinois, for several days. The spectacle of northern whites engaged in such violent tactics spurred the organization of a group to press for racial justice. By that time there was already sentiment within the black community against the policies of Booker T. Washington for accommodation with white power in the South. Led by W.E.B. Du Bois, a longtime critic of Washington with a Ph.D. from Harvard, blacks met in Niagara Falls, Canada, in 1905 to explore ways in which to reduce racism and injustice. In 1906, Dubois said: 'In the past year the work of the Negro hater has flourished in the land' [26 *p. 146*].

The reaction to the Springfield riots led a Socialist named William English Walling to summon white and black reformers to examine what could be done to improve the situation of black Americans. They gathered in early 1909 and created what became the National Association for the Advancement of Colored People (NAACP). Their goals were to rid the nation of segregation, to protect the right to vote, and to see that the Fourteenth and Fifteenth Amendments were enforced. Though never part of the main thrust of progressive reform, the crusade for racial equality would prove to be one of the more persistent legacies of the period [26; 75].

By the end of the first decade of the new century, the campaign for woman suffrage had regained momentum after years of difficulty and slow progress. Reaching out to college women through meetings aimed at their concerns, the leaders of the National American Woman Suffrage Association began to attract 'a wealthy and respectable class of women into comfortable participation in suffrage.' Membership stood at 12,000 in 1906. It would reach 117,000 four years later. Like other interest groups of the Progressive Era, the advocates of woman suffrage were organizing in a concerted way to press their political demands. Whether this gradualistic strategy would suit the more radical members of the movement would become an issue in the years ahead [95 *p. 51*].

Within both major political parties, divisions between progressive and conservative wings were becoming more pronounced. Among the Democrats, the emerging distinction was between those who wanted to use the power of the government to address social problems and those who clung to the older states-rights position that had characterized the Democrats since the Civil War. William Jennings Bryan, the likely nominee again in 1908, leaned more to the side of wielding government power. No Democrat spoke of turning government authority to the issue of race relations in the South to improve the lot of black people, but there were tensions over the extent to which the power of the state should pursue social justice.

THE PRESIDENTIAL CONTEST IN 1908

In 1908 the Democrats gave Bryan a third chance to win the presidency. Heavier and less handsome than when he made his appearance in national politics in 1896, Bryan retained the ability to galvanize a Democratic audience with his religiously tinged appeal to moral values. The party thought that it had a reasonable chance for victory in 1908. The backing of organized labor was an asset, the party was united, and the Republicans had been in power a long time. Most of all, Theodore Roosevelt would not be on the ballot again. The divisions within the Republican party seemed even more pronounced than those that the Democrats faced. 'To be suspected of disloyalty to Bryan in those days,' said one reporter, 'was almost like buying a ticket to private life' [43 *p. 38*].

The dominant fact for the Republicans as 1908 neared was the determination of Theodore Roosevelt to have a decisive role in picking the party's nominee. He now regretted his election-night statement in 1904, and wished that he had never made it. Having issued such a pledge, however, he loyally adhered to it. What he was not prepared to do, however, was to step aside and let the Republicans work their own will. Roosevelt knew that such a course would probably result in the selection of a conservative who would not extend the president's legislative or administrative legacy. That Roosevelt could not allow [28].

By 1906 the friction between Republican progressives, as they more and more styled themselves, and those who were known as 'standpatters' (after the term in draw poker where one 'stands-pat' with a good hand), conservatives, or the Old Guard, became even more pronounced. Younger men in the party, eager to make their way politically, were more likely to become progressives, but otherwise the split came between those who favored moderate reform and those who did not. Especially in the Middle West, the battle lines between the two factions were sharply drawn. In Iowa, Wisconsin, Kansas, Indiana, and Minnesota, the struggles between progressive and conservative factions reached open political warfare. 'There is pretty wide dissatisfaction and more factions and division that I have ever known in the Republican party in years gone by,' was the verdict of a Kansas party member during the spring of 1908 [28 *p. 96*].

Within this context of party division, Theodore Roosevelt sought to find a nominee to his liking among the field of possible Republican contenders. Neither of the two leading progressive hopefuls, Governor Charles Evans Hughes of New York or Senator Robert M. La Follette of Wisconsin, shared Roosevelt's attitudes on issues or were deferential enough to the president's leadership. Instead, Roosevelt turned to his own Secretary of War, William Howard Taft, as the best choice to extend the legacy of what Roosevelt and his allies called 'my policies.' Taft seemed to be a devoted adherent of Roosevelt's approach to governing. In fact, the two men had rarely explored their philosophical differences about the presidency or the reach of national power [65].

Adding to Taft's appeal to Roosevelt was his base in Ohio. If Taft won the nomination, it would undercut the standing of the senator from that state, Joseph B. Foraker, who was the leading critic of Roosevelt's handling of the Brownsville episode. By the late winter of 1907 Roosevelt was a virtual campaign manager for Taft, and was using presidential influence to line up delegates for his Cabinet colleague [76].

The result was a first ballot nomination for Taft in June 1908. However, both Roosevelt and Taft were unable to prevent the conservatives in their party from writing a platform that did not endorse many of the progressive ideas with which Roosevelt was associated. Both factions in the party looked to Taft to help them in the struggle that was raging in many states. That dilemma put more pressure on Taft, who had never run for state or national office before [28].

In the 1908 election, the Democrats began with high hopes for victory, but the resources and experience of the Republicans, combined with Roosevelt's personal leadership of the Taft campaign, carried the former Secretary of War to victory by 321 electoral votes to 162 for Bryan. While Taft demonstrated some ability as a campaigner, the key to his success was Roosevelt. The rest of the party experienced some losses to the Democrats in state governor races and in a drop off of votes for Republican candidates running with Taft. Clearly it would require a high degree of political skill on Taft's part to keep his party together [28; 40].

Almost as soon as victory was achieved, the Taft–Roosevelt alliance began to show signs of friction. The Taft family wanted the president-elect to be 'his own king' and to demonstrate independence from Roosevelt. The men around the out-going president were looking for any signs that Taft might be less than loyal to the Roosevelt legacy. During the months between Taft's election in November 1908 and his inauguration in March 1909, the two camps became even more suspicious of each other's motives and purposes [28].

For Roosevelt the last months of his term produced a bruising battle with Congress where Republican conservatives at last saw a chance to get even with the president for his harsh treatment of them during the preceding seven years. In this struggle, the people sided with the president and his popularity rose to new heights. As Roosevelt planned a safari to Africa that would take him out of the country for a year, commentators joked that Wall Street was hoping 'that a lion would do its duty.' That wry remark indicated how much Roosevelt had done to reshape business–government relations during his nearly two terms in the White House. He had made reform respectable and given it an important momentum for his successor. It was not clear, however, how much William Howard Taft would extend and build upon the example that Roosevelt had laid down [*Doc. 13*].

CHAPTER FOUR

PROGRESSIVISM AT ITS HEIGHT

Between the time when Theodore Roosevelt left for a safari in Africa in March 1909 and the election of Woodrow Wilson to the presidency in November 1912, the United States went through a period of political upheaval. The Socialist party reached the apex of its electoral influence in the country, the Republicans divided into warring factions, and the Democrats ended their long period out of national power.

For the interest groups that were pursuing aspects of the progressive agenda these years saw significant gains. The woman suffrage movement gathered momentum with new, more militant approaches and the success of statewide organizing campaigns. In similar fashion, the Anti-Saloon League saw marked acceleration in the number of states and localities banning the sale of alcohol. Restriction of immigration, the outlawing of child labor, the drives for an income tax and the direct election of senators all drew nearer to victory during these tumultuous years.

The forces of change came together in 1912 with a presidential election that saw the strongest field of candidates in the nation's history and a vigorous debate about the direction and nature of reform. The bitter primary campaign between Theodore Roosevelt and William Howard Taft during the first half of 1912 produced a thorough airing of the differences within the Republican party over the scope of government regulation. The ensuing debate in the general election between Roosevelt and Wilson and their doctrines of the New Nationalism and the New Freedom showed how much progressivism had changed the nature of the dialogue about the reach and legitimacy of national power.

When the smoke of battle blew away, the Democrats were in control and the Republicans had been divided into progressive and conservative elements. The party system, while shaken, would reconstitute itself by 1914 and the outbreak of World War I. Nonetheless, the parties had redefined themselves along ideological lines that would have seemed improbable just five years earlier. In that sense, 1912 was a presidential contest that looked forward to the elections of the remainder of the twentieth century rather than backward to the ways in which Democrats and Republicans had contested for power during the last half of the preceding century.

TAFT AND HIS PROBLEMS

When William Howard Taft took the oath of office on 4 March 1909, Washington was buried in the midst of an unexpected blizzard. Beneath the surface, relations between Roosevelt and Taft were almost as chilly. The deterioration in their friendship was well under way by the time the two men parted after Taft had delivered his inaugural remarks. Roosevelt intended to leave the country for a year on a hunting trip in Africa. In that way, he believed, he would avoid charges that he was trying to run the White House from the shadows [28].

Taft brought to the presidency a different philosophy of the office than the one Roosevelt had used during his administration. Where Roosevelt had asserted that the president could take any action that was not expressly forbidden in the Constitution, Taft, a lawyer by training, insisted that there must be an explicit authority in the fundamental document for whatever the chief executive did. That meant that Taft would be less daring than Roosevelt had been. Away from the stimulating influence of Roosevelt's personality, Taft's natural conservatism on policy issues also came to the fore [40].

The new president faced a challenging political dilemma. The Republican party was split into progressive and conservative factions. The more reform-minded part of the party was not as strong in Congress as were the Republican conservatives. Thus Taft confronted the problem of how to deal with his party's leadership on Capitol Hill. If he challenged them, he would probably lose any hope of passing constructive legislation. Yet if he worked with men such as Speaker Joseph G. Cannon, he would be open to charges from the progressives that he was abandoning the Roosevelt tradition.

The problems that Taft faced required great political skill to work through, and that is where the new president proved wanting. The presidency was the first major elective office that Taft had sought, and he had few of the natural talents of a national politician. He refused to cultivate the Washington press corps, which was gaining in influence and importance, and he paid little attention to his own public image. Where Roosevelt had carefully kept his tennis playing out of public view, Taft played golf openly at a time when the sport was largely the preserve of the rich and privileged classes. A hard worker when he wanted to be, Taft could procrastinate, and sometimes did not prepare his speeches until the last minute, a trait that produced some public relations embarrassments [28; 40].

REVISING THE TARIFF

The first task that Taft faced was revision of the protective tariff. At a time before the income tax was adopted, the duties on goods coming into the United States formed the large part of national revenues. Customs duties had been high since the adoption of the Dingley Tariff Law in 1897. While Republicans associated the protective tariff with national prosperity, the Democrats had attacked the law as an element in the inflation that had become more pronounced since 1900. As a result, the Republicans had promised a 'revision' of tariff rates in their 1908 platform, but had not said whether revision would leave tariff rates higher or lower [28; 43].

Passing a tariff bill was an elaborate political ballet during the Progressive Era. First, the House of Representatives, where all revenue bills had to originate, adopted a bill. In 1909 the lower house, behind the chair of the Ways and Means Committee, Sereno E. Payne of New York, approved a bill that made reductions in tariff duties. The House could take that step because they knew that the real bill would be written after the Senate acted and a conference committee met to reconcile the competing versions of tariff policy.

In the Senate the leader of the Republicans, Nelson Aldrich of Rhode Island, crafted a bill that made concessions to conservatives and western senators by leaving rates close to what the Dingley law had done. That tactic aroused the anger of progressive Republican senators from the Middle West such as Robert La Follette of Wisconsin, Jonathan P. Dolliver of Iowa, and Albert J. Beveridge of Indiana. They attacked the Senate version as a sell-out of tariff reform and said that it violated progressive principles of openness, fairness to the consumer, and justice to the nation. The episode galvanized the reform element within the Republican party [28; 40; 43].

In the end, Taft intervened to have the Senate–House conference committee enact a measure closer to his vision of tariff reform. The resulting Payne–Aldrich Tariff of 1909 did not achieve the goal of lowering the tariff in any substantial degree, and anti-tariff elements among the Republicans were unhappy. In a speech at Winona, Minnesota, on 17 September 1909, Taft called the law 'the best tariff bill that had ever been passed.' This example of presidential exaggeration further alienated Taft from the progressive Republicans [28 *p. 119*].

THE BALLINGER–PINCHOT CONTROVERSY

More damaging to Taft in the long run was an argument that developed within the administration over the proper direction of conservation policy. Taking care of the nation's natural resources had been one of the major accomplishments of Roosevelt's presidency, and he looked to Taft to carry on that tradition. The main instrument for Roosevelt had been the Chief Forester, Gifford Pinchot, who had implemented Roosevelt's approach of strong executive supervision of resource issues. More than any other single person in the government, Pinchot embodied the 'Roosevelt policies' in action [10; 79; 83].

Taft and his Secretary of the Interior, Richard A. Ballinger, regarded with skepticism Roosevelt's expansive use of presidential authority to manage conservation questions. They believed, instead, that the president should only act where express authority existed for such executive decrees. These divergent views showed up during 1909 in a bureaucratic battle between Ballinger and Pinchot over a number of resource issues. One of these involved coal lands in Alaska. Pinchot began leaking anti-Ballinger information to his friends among reporters, and stories appeared suggesting that the Secretary of the Interior had sinister and dishonest motives for his rejection of the preferences of Pinchot and Roosevelt [10; 83].

This controversy had two unfortunate results for Taft and his presidency. It enhanced the impression that he was abandoning a progressive course and drawing closer to the conservatives. More important, by dealing with conservation issues in this way, he was challenging the Roosevelt legacy directly. News of Taft's decisions filtered back to Roosevelt in Africa on his safari. Since he and Taft were not communicating directly, their relationship deteriorated as their friends fed them misleading information about each other [28].

This controversy reached a climax in early 1910 when Pinchot wrote a letter to a senator attacking Ballinger's honesty and record in office. Faced with a clear act of insubordination against his administration, Taft had no choice but to fire Pinchot. The incident led to a congressional investigation that embarrassed the White House. The even more dangerous effect was to convince Roosevelt that Taft had indeed abandoned his legacy. Roosevelt said that now 'he had to admit that he had gone wrong on certain points; and then I also had to admit to myself deep down underneath I had known all along he was wrong, on points as to which I had tried to deceive myself by loudly proclaiming to myself that he was right' [3 *vol. VII, p. 80*].

THE REPUBLICANS DIVIDED

By the spring of 1910, the Taft administration was in deep political trouble. The fissure with Roosevelt was growing wider, and many progressives believed that the president should not be nominated for a second term. These tensions flared when the House of Representatives in March 1910 stripped Speaker Cannon of some of his powers. A combination of Democrats and progressive Republicans worked to limit Cannon's ability to block legislation of which he disapproved. The episode was seen as a victory for openness and reform generally, but Taft did not receive any of the credit because he had become so identified with the Speaker and the Republican conservatives [28; 43].

The Republican party was in a state of disarray. The customary unity and cohesion that had marked the party since the 1880s was less evident. The crucial dividing point was over the extent and reach of government power as a regulatory instrument. Roosevelt and the forces allied with him wanted to press forward with a program to enact what was coming to be called 'social justice.' Taft and the conservatives thought that the process of regulation had gone far enough and a pause was in order [24; 28; 40].

In one respect, Taft wanted to be more aggressive in using the law to enforce legislation than Roosevelt was. Taft believed in the vigorous enforcement of the Sherman Antitrust Act (1890) to break up monopoly power. His Justice Department filed more suits under the Sherman Act in four years than Roosevelt did in nearly eight. By this time, Roosevelt had come to believe that merely breaking up big business was not a wise policy. He preferred, as he had done as president, to encourage socially useful corporations through a process of mutual cooperation. Only in the case of clear corporate misbehavior should the Sherman Act come into play. Roosevelt was moving toward a version of progressivism that used the power of the national government to oversee businesses in what he regarded as the public interest. At the same time, Roosevelt was evolving a program of government action to address the social inequities of the United States.

When Roosevelt returned home in June 1910 after a year in Africa and a triumphant tour of European capitals, he told reporters that he was out of politics and would not be speaking on national issues. This burst of self-denial did not last very long. Within weeks, Roosevelt was engaged in carving out his own positions on issues of the day as a means of saving the Republican party from Taft and his policies. As he did so, he took progressive doctrines to a new level of sophistication and set the stage for the great debate of 1912 over the direction of American reform [24; 28; 40].

ROOSEVELT AND THE NEW NATIONALISM

During August 1910 Roosevelt made a speaking tour of the Middle West. The decisive moment came when he delivered a talk at Osawatomie, Kansas, on 31 August. The place was associated with the anti-slavery martyr John Brown, and Roosevelt gave the most radical speech of his career. It became known as the 'New Nationalism' speech. In it Roosevelt went beyond the Square Deal of his presidency to set out a new role for the government in dealing with social issues.

'The New Nationalism regards the executive power as the steward of the public welfare,' he told the huge crowd, and then he went on to develop his argument for a broader regulatory role for the national government. 'When I say that I am for the square deal, I mean not merely that I stand for fair play under the present rules of the game, but that I stand for having those rules changed so as to work for a more substantial equality of opportunity and reward for equally good service.' In other speeches, he charged that federal courts had hampered reform by preventing either the states or the national governments from regulating effectively. His indictment of the judiciary contributed to a feeling among many conservatives that Roosevelt had become a dangerous radical [*Doc. 9*; 28 *p. 128*].

The New Nationalism ideology represented a significant elaboration of one vein of American progressivism. It embodied Roosevelt's faith in the strong presidency, his commitment to a broader program of regulation, and a growing conviction that the nation must address the plight of women, children, and the underprivileged generally. Roosevelt did not include in his concerns the status of minorities. But his articulation of themes of justice, equality, and more power for the state looked forward to the goals of liberalism as they would emerge in Franklin D. Roosevelt's New Deal and Lyndon Johnson's Great Society [24; 28].

THE ELECTION OF 1910

Roosevelt's stance for his version of progressivism did not please conservative opinion within his own party. Many of Taft's friends, including Mabel Boardman, who was active in a number of charitable causes in Washington, believed that the president had not received proper credit for his legislative accomplishments. They resented Roosevelt's failure to praise Taft, or, as Boardman put it, 'it would seem as if the success of the President was a source of annoyance rather than a satisfaction to' Roosevelt [*Doc. 14*].

Roosevelt's new radicalism set off a running battle within the Republican ranks that further weakened the party's chances in the 1910 elections. After more than a decade of Republican congressional dominance, the American people were ready for a change and the Democrats found themselves the beneficiaries of this new spirit [43].

A number of issues worked against the Republican cause. One of these was inflation. Since 1900 the cost of living had risen and the higher prices had an impact on the wallets of working people and the middle class. These voters listened receptively to Democratic claims that the protective tariff was a major element in making the necessities of life more expensive. The Democrats also made productive use of the prohibition issue. The Republicans were more inclined to use the state to regulate social behavior such as drinking in 1910, and the Democrats identified themselves with the cause of personal liberty. In the South, the race issue was also used as orators denounced what might happen if Roosevelt's dream of a powerful central government came to fruition [28; 43].

The 1910 elections proved to be a Republican disaster and a Democratic triumph. The Republicans lost fifty-eight seats in the House and ten seats in the Senate. The Democrats made their biggest gains in the East, previously centers of Republican strength. In the statehouses across the country, Democrats were successful, especially in New Jersey where Woodrow Wilson, the president of Princeton University, capitalized on Republican divisions to win the gubernatorial race. Suddenly it appeared as if the Democrats might have a chance to win the White House in 1912 [43].

THE QUICKENING TEMPO OF REFORM

The first two years of Taft's presidency saw other progressive reforms gain in strength and followers. The woman suffrage movement experienced a surge in popularity as more states added themselves to the ranks of those allowing women to exercise the franchise. Prohibitionists added to the number of localities where the sale and manufacter of alcohol were eliminated. There was a sense in the air that reform had an irresistible momentum behind it.

For woman suffragists, the start of the second decade of the new century brought renewed optimism about their prospects. On the national level, the National Woman Suffrage Association (NAWSA) sent a petition with more than 400,000 signatures to Congress in 1910 asking for the right to vote. Meanwhile, younger and more militant suffragists turned to public demonstrations and reached out to the working class for support. State elections brought positive outcomes for the next two years. Washington State voted for suffrage in November 1910. California produced the same result a year later. Three more states – Arizona, Kansas, and Oregon – joined the suffrage ranks in 1912. However, campaigns faltered in Ohio, Wisconsin, and Michigan. More and more, campaigners turned their attention to achieving a national amendment to the Constitution. Above all, the suffrage workers felt a new energy animating their campaign. As one advocate put it in 1910, their movement 'is actually fashionable now. The lectures on suffrage, the benefits for suffrage, the articles about suffrage, ... are actually uncountable. It's lovely!' [*Doc. 17; 93; 95 p. 54*].

The prohibition movement also gathered momentum during these years. The main thrust of dry sentiment came in the South, where in state after state counties adopted local-option statutes that enabled them to ban liquor sales. Oklahoma went completely 'dry' in 1907. In Texas the issue of liquor control dominated politics. As time went on, however, the strategy of increasing the area of prohibition seemed too slow, especially in the parts of the country such as the Northeast where wet sentiment predominated. The Anti-Saloon League began lobbying for a law to prevent the shipment of liquor into prohibitionist states. They saw that as the prelude to a constitutional amendment to ban liquor altogether [*Doc. 7; 24; 53; 101*].

A third element of reform that gained attention during the Taft years was immigration restriction. The pace of immigration into the United States intensified during the first decade of the century. In 1907, for example, nearly 1.2 million newcomers entered the United States. The waves of immigrants heightened cultural and racial fears among the white, middle-class population, where ideas about Social Darwinism and Anglo-Saxon purity found a ready audience. Congress authorized the Dillingham Commission to look into the immigration issue in 1911 and that body produced restrictionist conclusions. Within the wing of the Democratic party strongest in the South and West and among progressive Republicans in Congress, there was growing sentiment for legislation to slow the flow of immigration. Roosevelt and Taft stood against such measures, but the tide in favor of restrictive laws was gaining strength [24].

Other events seemed to emphasize the need for society to address problems of the working class. In March 1911 the Triangle Shirtwaist Company fire in New York City saw a building in the garment district burst into flames. The women who worked inside in cramped and unsafe conditions raced for the windows and the inadequate exits. The death toll reached 146 women as they leaped to the pavement in the vain hope of survival. The New York legislature began a probe into the tragedy that laid the groundwork for remedial legislation. Led by Democrats Alfred E. Smith and Robert F. Wagner, who were associated with the party's machine, Tammany Hall, the lawmakers adopted fifty laws to insure fire safety and better working conditions [18; 24].

THE RACE FOR THE WHITE HOUSE IN 1912

The impending 1912 presidential race thus focused the attention of the two major parties and the Socialists on issues of reform and the role of government. Throughout 1911 contenders jockeyed for advantage in the race for the Democratic and Republican nominations. For the Republicans the imponderable element was Theodore Roosevelt. After the 1910 elections, he and President Taft had worked out an informal truce in their dispute over the party's future. For the first six months, something like peace settled on their relationship.

The only potential challenger to Taft's renomination was Senator La Follette of Wisconsin, who had established the National Progressive Republican League to promote his candidacy. La Follette enjoyed little support outside of his home state, and it was clear by the summer of 1911 that he was not a credible alternative to Taft for most Republicans. Roosevelt was the only reformer among the Republicans who had a serious chance to win [*Doc. 16*; 9; 28; 40].

On the Democratic side, the fresh face and the front-runner was Woodrow Wilson. In his early months as governor of New Jersey, he had been able to pass a program of corporate control through the legislature. With his southern background and northern base, Wilson was well-positioned to bring the two wings of his party together into a unified bloc. He made a number of speaking tours that further enhanced his national standing. Other contenders included the Speaker of the House, James Beauchamp 'Champ' Clark of Missouri, and Governor Judson Harmon of Ohio. The Democratic nomination became more and more attractive as Republican feuding resumed and the likelihood grew that Taft could not be re-elected in 1912 [63].

The Socialists under Eugene V. Debs also looked upon 1912 as a promising year for their cause. They had been able to elect a number of mayors in medium-sized cities, especially in Wisconsin, and the appeal of their critique of industrialism was growing in working-class districts. A problem for the third-party movement was the more radical wing of Socialism, led by the Industrial Workers of the World. Advocating violent overthrow of the existing social order through a general strike, the IWW gave conservatives a strong propaganda weapon to use against the Socialist movement as a whole. Nonetheless, the support that the IWW gave to free speech in the West made them a growing element on the left by 1912 [27; 70].

A major confrontation between capital and labor, led by the IWW, occurred in Lawrence, Massachusetts, in January 1912. Mill owners in this textile manufacturing town trimmed pay for their women workers. The result was a walkout of more than 20,000 workers. The IWW sent in organizers to assist the strikers. Despite martial law and violence sparked by the employers, the strikers gained sympathy as the public saw the plight of children forced out of their homes by the strike. The strong-arm tactics backfired on the employers and they had to make concessions to end the strike in March 1912. The volatility of labor relations was another element in the turbulent year that lay ahead [24; 27; 38].

TAFT AND ROOSEVELT SPLIT

The political landscape was shaken during the fall of 1911 when Roosevelt and Taft renewed their personal and policy battle. In late October the Justice Department filed an antitrust suit against United States Steel. The particulars of the case included the charge that the company had acted illegally when it acquired the Tennessee Coal and Iron Company during the Panic of 1907. Since Theodore Roosevelt had endorsed the acquisition at the time as a way of relieving the nation's financial distress, the allegation in the indictment was a direct rebuke to the former president. Roosevelt reacted angrily both publicly and privately to what the Taft administration seemed to be saying about his judgment of issues. He began to listen more sympathetically to those of his friends who were urging him to run for president in 1912. To be sure that he had a good chance to win, Roosevelt asked his associates to demonstrate that there was genuine popular support for his candidacy. Once that signal was sent, his allies had no difficulty in producing a flood of letters urging the former president to become a candidate [24; 28].

Events moved quickly in the winter of 1912. By the end of February Roosevelt released a letter to seven progressive Republican governors saying that he would be a candidate if the Republicans wanted him. He told reporters that 'my hat is in the ring, the fight is on, and I am stripped to the buff' [28 *p. 141*]. Roosevelt knew that he faced a difficult fight to overcome the natural power of Taft's incumbent status, but he was now convinced that his one-time friend had betrayed him. The only way to achieve vindication, to regain national power, and to keep himself fully busy was to become president for a third term.

Roosevelt had moved in a very progressive direction by the winter of 1912. When he spoke to the Ohio Constitutional Convention on 26 February, for example, he came out for allowing voters to overturn the decision of a state court by a recall election. That endeavor to undercut the ruling of a court seemed to Republican conservatives the clearest possible evidence that Roosevelt wanted to dominate the other branches of government. In an article that appeared in *The Independent* of New York on 28 March 1912, one conservative asked: 'Are we prepared to enter on a path which leads directly towards the Mexicanization of our country?'

Taft was distressed to see what Roosevelt had done, but he had no intention of standing aside. With the control of the Republican machinery that the White House possessed, Taft and his men fully expected to gain a renomination. Whether the nomination would be worth anything after a bruising fight with Roosevelt was another matter. Like so many Republicans, Taft now believed that Roosevelt's third-term ambitions made him a danger to the nation. Taft was prepared to wage all-out political war to deny Roosevelt the Republican nomination [24; 28].

The intraparty battle that followed during the winter and spring of 1912 was one of the legendary confrontations in the political history of the United States. Roosevelt knew that he could not win if he relied on the votes of the state party conventions where Taft dominated. His only realistic chance lay with the will of Republican voters themselves. Accordingly, Roosevelt and his campaign organization sought to use the relatively new device of the nominating primary to put their candidate before the voters. Only a few states used such a process in 1912, but wherever one occurred Roosevelt wanted to be entered.

At first the momentum of events went in Taft's direction as the conservatives among the Republicans rallied to the president. Roosevelt had to compete as well with Senator La Follette, who stayed in the race despite a general lack of enthusiasm for his candidacy. The Wisconsin senator had the effect of drawing away some votes from Roosevelt. Roosevelt was intent on staying in the race until the six states that had agreed to hold presidential primaries could be heard from [24; 28].

By the end of March Roosevelt knew that his only hope was to make a campaign on his own. He carried Illinois, with its fifty-six delegates, on 9 April, and then won in Pennsylvania four days later. Roosevelt won three additional states in April, while Taft did well in non-primary states such as Michigan and Indiana. The result seemed likely to turn on primaries in Massachusetts and Ohio.

By now the bitterness of the contest had become intense. No longer friends, Taft and Roosevelt went at each other with no holds barred. They exchanged attacks on their personal and political integrity. Taft said of Roosevelt's attacks: 'I was a man of straw; but I have been a man of straw long enough; every man who has blood in his body and who has been mis-represented as I have been is forced to fight.' Roosevelt told friends that Taft 'means well, but means well feebly, and has neither vision nor broad social sympathy' [3 *vol. VII, p. 532* (second quotation); 28 *p. 144*].

Taft staved off defeat when he carried the Massachusetts primary in a narrow victory. Nonetheless, Roosevelt swept through the primaries in Ohio, New Jersey, and Maryland, and the nomination was still in doubt when the delegates gathered in Chicago for the Republican National Convention. Roosevelt had some 411 committed delegates, short of the 540 needed for victory. La Follette and other minor candidates controlled about fifty votes. On paper, Taft had only 201 delegates, but that understated his strength. Of the 166 uninstructed delegates, most were leaning to Taft. Another 254 delegates were contested between Taft and Roosevelt, and most of them were likely to be allocated to Taft because he controlled the Republican National Committee that handled seating of disputed delegates. There was no clear winner as the Convention neared, but Taft had the advantage of controlling the party machinery [24; 28].

That asset proved to be decisive for Taft when the Republicans met in Chicago in June 1912. The Republican National Committee assigned 239 of the 254 disputed delegates to the president and with that settled his nomination was assured. An angry Roosevelt asked his delegates to leave the hall and he told them that they should come back to Chicago later that summer to create an alternative Republican party or a third party altogether. Their goal should be 'to nominate for the presidency a Progressive on a Progressive platform.' The remnant of the Republicans renominated Taft for a second term, though by now the president knew that he had almost no chance of victory [28 *p. 147*].

THE RISE OF WOODROW WILSON

With the Republicans split into angry factions, the Democrats had a superb opportunity to win the presidency for the first time in a generation. They needed, however, to select an attractive, reform-minded candidate or Roosevelt might pull together progressives from both parties into a winning coalition. That consideration gave the edge to the party's front-runner, Woodrow Wilson. During 1911 Wilson had shown strength across the country, but as 1912 began and the Democratic nomination seemed worth more in the wake of Republican feuding, his candidacy stalled [34; 43].

The main challenger to Wilson was the Speaker of the House, Champ Clark, who appealed to conservatives and moderates. To many Democrats Wilson was an unknown quantity who had come late to reform. That was true. As late as 1908 Wilson had been suspicious of William Jennings Bryan. But as governor of New Jersey Wilson had moved toward progressivism and he knew that identification with change was his best approach to the White House. By 1912 Wilson was identified with regulation of corporations, a lower tariff, and political reforms such as the initiative and referendum [43].

As the most progressive candidate in the Democratic field, Wilson enjoyed latent strength in every region of the country. That asset proved to be crucial when the Democrats met at Baltimore in late June 1912. Though Champ Clark achieved a majority vote on several ballots, he never approached the two-thirds needed for the Democratic nomination. Once it became clear that Clark could not win, Wilson's position as the most plausible progressive asserted itself. On the 46th ballot he was nominated and a united Democratic party prepared for victory.

Wilson's nomination undercut Roosevelt's third-party strategy since it was unlikely that progressive Democrats would bolt their ticket for Roosevelt. Nonetheless, having repudiated Taft, Roosevelt had no choice but to press forward. He and his allies called for Republicans sympathetic to him to meet in Chicago in August to form a third party. What became the Progressive party was an assemblage of old-line politicians who did not like Taft, modern reformers who saw Roosevelt as their champion, social workers who hoped to write a platform dealing with their special causes, and individuals moved by Roosevelt's celebrity and charisma [24; 28; 40].

The convention was a combination of revival meeting, old-time convention, and pep rally for Roosevelt. Delegates adopted 'Onward Christian Soldiers' as their theme song. Their platform was the most advanced that a major American political party had ever adopted. It advocated woman suffrage, limits on the power of judges, the pending constitutional amendment for an income tax, restrictions on child labor, the minimum wage for women, and a program of social insurance that looked forward to Social Security. Progressives believed that 'an enlarged measure of social and industrial justice' was an imperative. The Progressive party did not go as far as the New Deal of Franklin D. Roosevelt would, but it represented a long step in that direction [*Doc. 18*; 24; 28 *p. 157*].

The key aspect of the Progressive approach, however, was Roosevelt's advocacy of what he called 'a strong, fundamental, administrative commission' that would provide 'permanent, active supervision' over businesses in interstate commerce. Roosevelt did not support abandoning enforcement of the Sherman Antitrust Act completely, but he did anticipate that the government and socially beneficial corporations would work together in the national interest as Roosevelt believed they had done during his second presidential term. By 1912, Roosevelt had taken the regulatory, bureaucratic aspect of the progressive movement to a degree of governmental activism that would have seemed unthinkable just a few years earlier. His program of the New Nationalism was a potent doctrine in the reform-minded atmosphere of 1912 [4; 28 *p. 157*; 40].

For Roosevelt to implement his ambitious program for the Progressive party required that he win the presidency in 1912. The Progressives did what they could to enhance their chances. Roosevelt's running mate was Governor Hiram Johnson of California, a hero to western reformers. Roosevelt also played down the race issue to try and attract white Democrats in the South. There was enough money to make a campaign, and Roosevelt himself planned to throw his prodigious energies into the struggle.

THE NEW NATIONALISM AND THE NEW FREEDOM

If the Democrats stayed united behind Wilson, however, Roosevelt had little realistic chance of victory. Sensing their first chance at the White House in twenty years, the Democrats looked to Wilson for a campaign theme that would offset Roosevelt's popular appeal. The candidate gave them what they needed when he enunciated, with the aid of Louis D. Brandeis, what came to be called the New Freedom. Faced with the results of the Progressive party convention, Wilson realized that he could not simply run as a conventional Democrat and leave Roosevelt's challenge unanswered [43].

He worked with a Boston lawyer named Louis D. Brandeis to frame a Democratic alternative. Known as the 'People's Attorney,' Brandeis had been arguing for years that bigness in business was against the interests of American consumers. Large firms, he maintained, curbed individual liberty and were also inefficient in their operations. The best thing government could do was to use the antitrust laws to break up concentrations of economic power. Competition among businessmen would insure that monopoly would not prevail. As Brandeis put the question to Wilson in 1912, the issue for the American people was 'Shall we have regulated competition or regulated monopoly?' [24; 28; 81 *pp. 108, 110*].

Brandeis's answer, which Wilson called the 'New Freedom,' gave the Democratic candidate just what he needed to meet Roosevelt's arguments on the campaign trail. Wilson now had a way of saying that Roosevelt's acceptance of bigness made the Progressive candidate the instrument of big business. Wilson charged that Roosevelt and big business were working together and that any regulation, or administrative agency, would become the pawn of large corporations. Wilson termed what Roosevelt proposed 'paternalism' [24; 81].

As a Democrat, Wilson had to find a way to be against corporate power and expanded regulation at the same time. What Brandeis proposed met Wilson's needs. Southern Democrats would oppose a government strong enough to regulate business because that same government might have the power to allow blacks to vote in the South. So Wilson confined himself to denunciations of the effects of corporate influence such as industrial accidents, child labor, and overcrowded cities. He did not suggest that government might address these problems directly. The New Freedom was a vague blueprint for governing, but an excellent weapon in the campaign [29].

The dispute between Roosevelt's New Nationalism and Wilson's New Freedom in 1912 posed a classic choice for progressives. In dealing with social problems, how much should an activist regulatory government try to accomplish? Roosevelt said that the nation must go further in the direction of government supervision. Wilson countered that there were ways to achieve Roosevelt's aims without broadening government power to the extent that the former president advocated. The enforcement of existing laws such as the Sherman Act, Wilson contended, would be all that was necessary [24; 29; 40].

The argument between these two candidates showed how far the nation had moved in the direction of progressive ideas by 1912. Programs for social justice that would have been deemed impossibly intrusive into private affairs in 1890 were now on the national agenda. The 1912 election set the terms of debate on domestic issues for decades to come.

While Roosevelt and Wilson exchanged ideas about the proper balance of progressive change, the other two major candidates took very different approaches to the campaign. President Taft observed the custom that incumbent chief executives should not campaign. Since he had no chance to win and the Republicans were short of funds, there was little else he could do but hope that Roosevelt would be beaten. Most conservative Republicans preferred that Roosevelt be defeated, even if it meant a Democratic victory.

Eugene V. Debs, on the other hand, made his usual energetic campaign to reach voters alienated by the Republicans and Democrats. He had more money, about $150,000 for the campaign, and a larger base in the country

1. By the second decade of the twentieth century, the drive for woman suffrage was gaining national momentum. A key event was the suffrage parade on 3 March 1913 in Washington, D.C. that managed to compete in popular attention with Woodrow Wilson's inauguration the next day. The heckling and sporadic violence to which the marchers were subjected attested to the passions that the suffrage issue aroused in Progressive Era America (Milstein Division of U.S. History, Local History and Genealogy, The New York Public Library, Astor, Lenox and Tilden Foundations.)

Bernard Partridge

Plate 2: Theodore Roosevelt's years in the American West and his heroism during
the Spanish-American War in 1898 shaped his image as a masculine leader of the
nation. The cartoonist depicts him here with his Rough Rider hat, mounted on a
spirited horse, to catch the aggressive patriotism that his career embodied.

Plate 3: When Theodore Roosevelt contended for the Republication nomination in 1912, it provided rich material for cartoonists in and out of the United States. Here a British cartoonist shows the former friends battling to keep each other from getting on the White House express while Roosevelt's big stick falls to the platform. The 1912 nomination contest remains one of the most memorable in the history of presidential elections.

Now, Mr. Railroadman, stock watering must stop—

Rates are too high—

They must come down—

Safety must be guaranteed—

I hope I impress my meaning on you—

Good day!"

RAILROAD LEGISLATION

From *Collier's Weekly*

Plate 4: Theodore Roosevelt's vigorous style of executive leadership provided much fodder for American cartoonists. During the battle over railroad regulation that produced the Hepburn Act in 1906, the president pressed rail executives for action. In this cartoon, Roosevelt's displeasure with stock manipulation and high rates, combined with his restless energy, overawes a 'railroadman'.

Plate 5: Woodrow Wilson's political appeal combined reform and a stern sense of moral values. From a background in higher education as President of Princeton University and then as Governor of New Jersey, he brought the Democrats back to the White House in 1912 after sixteen years of Republican rule. During his first two years in office, Wilson pursued the program of change he dubbed 'The New Freedom'.

Plate 6: Jane Addams symbolized the crucial role of women in social change during the Progressive Era. As the founder of the settlement home, Hull House, in Chicago, she was a forerunner of a generation of reformers who endeavored to improve the lives of residents of the growing cities.

Theodore Roosevelt's Labor Record

Does Labor Get a Square Deal?
It has from Theodore Roosevelt!

As Member of the New York State Assembly he voted for 20 Important Labor Measures

Published by

National Progressive Party

Hotel Manhattan   **New York City**

Plate 7: When Theodore Roosevelt ran for president as the candidate of the Progressive Party in 1912, he made a strong appeal to labor as part of his emphasis on social justice. The cover of one of the millions of pamphlets that were distributed in that election underscores that Roosevelt's sympathy for working men and women went back to when he first served in the New York Assembly during the 1880s.

Plate 8: The Republicans relied on the protective tariff as their main electoral theme throughout the Progressive Era. This pamphlet supporting Taft in 1912 asked the voters to remember the hard times of the 1890s under Grover Cleveland and to contrast it with Republican prosperity during the first decade of the twentieth century. The appeal did not work against Woodrow Wilson and the Democrats in 1912.

since the Socialists claimed 135,000 dues-paying members in 1912. Debs drew sizeable crowds, though no one expected him to win. In the end the Socialists drew their highest total ever, more than 900,000 ballots. With 6 percent of the vote, Debs had brought Socialism to the edge of political respectability. There was an audience for even more radical answers in 1912 [70].

The outcome of the election saw Wilson and the Democrats capitalize on Republican divisions to regain the White House and control of both houses of Congress. Wilson received nearly 6.3 million popular ballots and he won 435 electoral votes. Roosevelt tallied 4.2 million votes and won 88 electoral votes. Taft trailed with 3.4 million votes and only 8 electoral votes. Wilson was still a minority president with just under 42 percent of the total vote [28].

One of the anomalies of this election that attracted four of the most qualified presidential candidates of the century was that it did not intensify popular interest in the campaign. The rate at which voters turned out in the North, for example, fell off some 12 percent from 1908. Wilson ran behind Bryan's total four years earlier, and the combined vote for Taft and Roosevelt lagged behind what Taft had polled in 1908. Even at its height of influence and power, progressivism was showing signs of losing its attraction to the American electorate [104].

For the moment, the question was whether Woodrow Wilson could make the Democrats into a party that could govern the United States. The Republicans assumed that the opposition would falter, as it had done under Grover Cleveland in the 1890s. Wilson was an unknown quantity as he and the Democrats celebrated their stunning victory. Progressives believed that the nation had more to do on the agenda of social justice, and they looked with expectancy at the New Freedom for answers [*Doc. 19*].

CHAPTER FIVE

PROGRESSIVISM IN DECLINE

For almost two years after the election of 1912, progressivism continued to define the political agenda of the United States. The outbreak of World War I in Europe during the summer of 1914 brought that situation to an end, and transformed the nature of partisan debate for the remainder of the decade. Once the United States had declared its neutrality in the conflict, questions of whether to intervene in Europe, the proper role for a neutral in the wake of the submarine weapon, and the shape of peace after the fighting stopped introduced new elements that accelerated some reforms and stifled others. The start of World War I thus marks a basic shift in American public life and the end of progressivism in its essentially domestic phase.

By the middle of 1914, the spirit of reform, which had been so evident since Theodore Roosevelt's second term, was showing signs of wear and tear. The Republican party had bounced back from the defeat of 1912 and anticipated large gains in the congressional elections in the fall. The Democrats under Wilson had shifted to the right and were trying to convince businessmen of the party's reliability and safety. The Progressive party that Roosevelt had launched in 1912 was withering away as its members returned to their Republican roots. The war disrupted this process of conservative revival for several years and changed the prospects for President Wilson in 1916.

REFORMS ADOPTED

Before Woodrow Wilson took office in March 1913, two reforms reached fruition that would have important effects on public policy and the selection of political candidates for the rest of the century. The Sixteenth Amendment to the Constitution was ratified in February 1913 when the final states gave their approval to the change. Tariff reformers had been lobbying for an amendment for years as a way of providing revenue for the government to offset reductions in customs duties. The main obstacle that they confronted was the Supreme Court's decision in 1895 in the case of

Pollock v. *Farmer's Loan and Trust* that ruled an income tax unconstitutional. In 1908 the Democratic platform called for an amendment to make the tax legal, and in the struggle over the Payne–Aldrich Tariff of 1909 an agreement was reached to submit an income tax amendment to the states. The Democratic gains in the elections of 1910 and 1912 provided the party with control of the legislatures in such key states as New York and New Jersey. That helped to produce the final victory. It remained to be seen how Congress would implement its new power. Few politicians in 1913 saw the income tax as a means of funding expansive social programs. Its main purpose was as an element in the debate over the place of the tariff in raising government revenue. The enactment and adoption of the income tax amendment, however, proved to be one of the most important and long-lasting achievements of the reform period. The rise of the social welfare programs of the twentieth century would not have been possible without the funding mechanism of the income tax.

The Seventeenth Amendment calling for the direct election of senators had not taken as long as the income tax to become part of the Constitution. For some time there had been complaints from reformers that having the individual state legislatures choose the senators allowed men with wealth and power to buy a seat in the upper house. Often it was only a matter of securing the votes of about half of the lawmakers in the majority party to decide the result. During the period from 1893 to 1902 the House of Representatives had on five occasions adopted a constitutional amendment calling for the direct election of senators. In each instance, the matter had died in the Senate, where members had a stake in perpetuating the existing arrangement. In the meantime, the practice of holding statewide preference primaries to indicate where the voters stood, which the legislatures were then required to follow, had been adopted in twenty-nine states by 1912. Then an unseemly scandal involving credible allegations of bribery in the Illinois legislature over the election of Republican William Lorimer in 1910–11 added momentum to the cause of reform. The Senate did not seat Lorimer and then adopted the amendment in June 1911. Ratification by the states followed quickly, and the amendment went into effect on 31 May 1913. The elections of 1914 would be the first where the new system would exist in every state. Advocates of the change predicted that the influence of money and corporate power would be reduced when the people had a chance to speak at the ballot box [19].

PROHIBITION AND WOMAN SUFFRAGE

In the days immediately preceding Wilson's inauguration, the fate of other reform proposals was much in the news. Prohibitionists achieved passage of the Webb–Kenyon Act in February 1913. The Senate agreed with the House that it should be illegal to transport liquor in interstate commerce from a jurisdiction where drinking was permitted to one where it was not. Although President William Howard Taft vetoed the bill in the waning days of his administration, the House and Senate quickly passed the measure again over his veto. The victory indicated the growing strength of the drys in the political arena. Their next plan was to push for a constitutional amendment to make the United States a dry nation [100].

On the day before Wilson was inaugurated, 3 March 1913, he arrived in Washington to prepare to take office. Unlike the presidents at the end of the twentieth century, he came down on the train from New Jersey with his family and without an elaborate security detail or entourage. To his surprise, he found that the people who were supposed to greet him had left to witness a parade of 5,000 woman suffrage advocates march up Pennsylvania Avenue. The parade was the idea of two young militant members of the suffrage movement, Alice Paul and Lucy Burns, who had enlisted the committee on congressional relations of the National American Woman Suffrage Association in their cause. These two women believed in direct action and public confrontation in the manner of the suffragettes in England at the same period [93; 95].

The parade attracted an angry crowd of spectators who yelled at the demonstrators and taunted them with insults. One newspaper account said that 'the women had to fight their way from the start and took more than one hour in making the first ten blocks.' Police, cavalry troops, and sympathetic male onlookers had to clear a path for the marchers. The result was a wave of sympathy and favorable publicity for the suffrage movement. Petitions poured into Washington asking that women be granted the vote and the members of NAWSA saw the prospects for a constitutional amendment improve. Meanwhile, Alice Paul and Lucy Burns created their own national organization, the Congressional Union, and began publishing their own magazine, *The Suffragist*. This split in the woman's suffrage movement was to have large consequences [93 p. 257].

WILSON AS PRESIDENT

The accession of Woodrow Wilson to the presidency on 4 March 1913 provided a stirring climax to these events. A skilled orator who wrote his own speeches, Wilson used the occasion to enunciate his vision of where the country should be going under the new Democratic mandate. 'This is not a day of triumph,' the new president said, 'it is a day of dedication. Men's hearts wait upon us; men's lives hang in the balance; men's hopes call upon us to say what we will do.' He spoke of the social costs of industrialism in graphic and moving language that summed up what his generation was trying to achieve. More than any other national figure of the Progressive

Era, Woodrow Wilson had the ability to articulate the goals of change in language that moved his followers to action [*Doc. 20*; *24 p. 193*].

The new president would prove to be one of the most interesting and complex personalities ever to serve in the White House. He had risen from a college presidency to the highest office in the land with dizzying speed, and he was a person convinced of his own destiny. He once told a friend that God had ordained that he should become President of the United States. Running for office, he had promised to pursue the 'common counsel' of wise advisers. Yet in office he proved to be one of the most isolated presidents in American history. He relied on a few intimate friends such as the honorary Texas 'colonel' Edward M. House, and worked with the very small presidential staff that was customary in those days. Wilson rarely read the newspapers and treated politicians with studied politeness that left many in his own party convinced that the president looked down on them [24; 28; 61].

Wilson's moralistic style as president made him very effective with those who shared his positions on public issues. Republicans considered him a hypocritical figure who often, as he put it, 'shaded the truth' to serve his own ends. Theodore Roosevelt and Henry Cabot Lodge regarded Wilson as unreliable and weak on foreign policy issues. For Roosevelt, Wilson was a weak president like Thomas Jefferson or James Buchanan. Rumors circulated in Washington of an intimate friendship with a woman named Mary Allen Hulbert Peck that had cast a shadow over Wilson's marriage before he became governor of New Jersey. The truth of the relationship is elusive, but Wilson's enemies did not trust him or regard him as sincere in either his public or personal life. His status as a minority president made many in the Republican party skeptical of his legitimacy to hold the nation's highest office. These cross-currents did not disrupt Wilson's first term; they proved more damaging in his second.

The Wilson administration had a very southern tone to it, and a number of articles appeared about how 'The South Was In the Saddle Again' for the first time since the Civil War had begun. Four members of Wilson's Cabinet came from the South, and three of these men were from Texas, where Colonel House found talent in his adopted city of Austin for the new president. Postmaster General Albert S. Burleson, Secretary of Agriculture David F. Houston, and soon Attorney General Thomas Watt Gregory received their Cabinet portfolios because of House's influence. In Congress, southerners benefited from the one-party system of their region to acquire seniority that in turn led to chairmanships of key committees. The dominance that southerners exerted in Congress stirred sectional animosities among the Republican minority on Capitol Hill [24; 28].

The losers in this shift were black Americans. Wilson had done some mild courting of the African-American vote in 1912, but once in office he deferred to the racial prejudices that he shared with his southern colleagues. Postmaster General Albert S. Burleson insisted that segregation should be the rule in his department, while Secretary of the Treasury William G. McAdoo sought to restrict black employees to segregated branches and divisions. The president claimed that 'Segregation is not humiliating but a benefit.' During its first two years, the Wilson administration drastically reduced the employment opportunities for African Americans in the federal government. The administration did not adopt the extreme views of some southern Democrats who wanted the Fourteenth and Fifteenth Amendments repealed, but reform for many in the Democratic party was strictly a program for whites only [77 *p. 391*].

Because of circulatory problems and a history of small strokes, Wilson tried very hard not to overtax himself as he carried out the duties of the presidency. As a result, he did his work as president in a relatively few hours daily, and then sought relaxation with his wife, daughters, and female kinfolk with whom he liked to spend time. A rapid writer and efficient worker, Wilson achieved a great deal within the limits that he imposed on himself.

A strong believer in his own religious faith, Wilson approached most issues from a moralistic point of view. Men were either his friends or his enemies; there was little in the way of middle ground. He once told a colleague that there were two sides to every question – a right side and a wrong side. When the tide of public opinion was with Wilson, as it was for his first two years, he could catch the popular mood in his language and tactics. Later in his presidency, when events did not run his way, he faced imposing difficulties, as in his advocacy of the League of Nations in 1918–19.

ENACTING THE NEW FREEDOM

At the outset of his presidency, however, the political scene could not have been more favorable to Wilson and the Democrats. The split among Republicans in 1912 had allowed the Democrats to win control of both houses of Congress with substantial majorities. Especially in the House, where more than a third of the Democratic members were freshmen, the new Democratic representatives knew that they owed their success to Wilson's presidential candidacy, and they were ready to do the bidding of the White House on such issues as lowering the tariff, creating a central bank, and regulating corporations. Although the Speaker of the House, Champ Clark, resented the way Wilson had won the nomination in 1912, he was eager to cooperate with the first Democratic president in two decades [24; 28].

The opposition was also demoralized and ineffective. The Republicans had not yet recovered from their stinging, unexpected loss in 1912, and there was a small contingent of Progressive representatives in the Congress as well that might sympathize with some of Wilson's programs. The nation was ready to see if the Democrats could defy their reputation for political ineptitude and become the vehicle to govern responsibly and implement the agenda of reform. If Wilson could avoid a repetition of the disasters that had overtaken Grover Cleveland during the 1890s, he had a chance to rehabilitate the reputation of the Democrats as a governing party.

The first priority was lowering the tariff, a subject on which the Democrats were in general unity. Wilson got the process off to an innovative start when he decided to address the lawmakers in person, the first president to do so since Thomas Jefferson abandoned the practice in 1801. He said that he wished to demonstrate that the chief executive was 'not a mere department of the Government hailing Congress from some isolated island of jealous power ... but a human being trying to cooperate with other human beings in a common service.' The step proved to be an important change in the way that presidents interacted with Congress and the public at large. Wilson had given future presidents a method of appealing to the public over the head of the lawmakers in dramatic fashion. In the process the State of the Union message, which had been a dry experience of hearing a bored clerk read aloud what the president had to say, became an event that took on greater importance as the twentieth century progressed [24 p. 194].

The actual process of securing tariff reduction was not as difficult for Wilson and his party as some Democrats had anticipated when the special session commenced. The conditions that had defeated Cleveland in 1894 no longer obtained. By 1912, the major industries in the United States had matured to the point that the protective tariff was not a large element in their business decisions. Government encouragement of their growth was helpful but not essential. They could view the prospect of lower tariff rates serenely and not mount a major lobbying campaign to affect the outcome of the tariff-writing process. The bulk of pro-tariff sentiment remained among smaller firms who had difficulty in lobbying effectively in Washington. Accordingly, it was not as risky in a political sense to be for lower rates as it would have been twenty years earlier [28].

Nonetheless, the process of passing what became the Underwood Tariff took up much of the time of Wilson's first year as president. The bill, named after Oscar W. Underwood of Alabama, chair of the House Ways and Means Committee, cleared the House by early May. It reduced rates on raw wool and sugar, and trimmed duties on consumer products such as woolens and cotton goods. Many food products were put on the free list, which meant that importers paid no duties on them at all. The lost revenue for the government would be made up by the adoption of an income tax. It levied a small tax on incomes above $4,000, with rising rates on incomes above $20,000. At a time when most industrial workers earned less than $1,000 annually, the income tax affected very few individuals. It did not seem at that time as if a major change in how the federal government financed the people's business had taken place [24].

The Democrats expected trouble for the bill in the Senate, but the process turned out to be smoother than Wilson and his party had anticipated. The president made a highly publicized attack on what he called an 'industrious' and 'insidious' lobbying effort to thwart the bill, coupled with a proposal that he would be the people's lobbyist. The move did not really affect the outcome. The Democrats remained unified for the most part, and Republican delaying tactics did not derail the majority. The Senate actually lowered duties and the Underwood Tariff was adopted in early October [28 *pp. 168–9*].

Because of World War I and its effect in disrupting the customary patterns of international trade, the Underwood Tariff never really had the chance to operate under normal conditions. The bill became historically important as the start of the income tax and as evidence that the Democrats could enact a credible legislative program. The Wilson administration had cleared the first obstacle to success. Now the party could turn to the pressing issue of reshaping the banking system.

REFORMING THE BANKING SYSTEM

Following the Panic of 1907 when J.P. Morgan had personally intervened to prop up the financial system, reformers of all persuasions had recognized the need to establish a central bank to manage the monetary affairs of the nation. Ever since Andrew Jackson had destroyed the Second Bank of the United States in the 1830s, the American economy had functioned without the kind of banking management that had become an accustomed part of the economy in European countries. Within the banking community the clamor for change had been building for more than a decade, but the 1907 episode, with the key role that J.P. Morgan as a private banker responsible only to himself played in resolving the crisis, underlined the need to do something about preventing a future disaster for the government and the economy [72].

By 1913 all shades of economic opinion within the major parties recognized that some form of central bank would be required to see that money was available in all parts of the nation as needed and that an adequate supply of currency was provided for the economy itself. The big question was whether the central bank would be under private or public authority. Eastern bankers naturally wanted a private institution where their interests would have a large influence. The Democrats of the South and West, suspicious of Wall Street, insisted that public control must be established.

Under the tutelage of Louis D. Brandeis and at the urging of Bryan, Wilson came out for public control in June 1913 [24; 28].

That was the important decision. After that issue was settled, the administration used its control of the Democratic caucus in Congress to see to it that a bill was framed that met what Wilson wanted. The Federal Reserve Act, which became law on 27 December 1913, set up a system of a Federal Reserve Board, twelve regional reserve banks, and the makings of a modern central banking system. The New Freedom had achieved one of its primary goals, and the Federal Reserve Act became the most important legacy of the presidency of Woodrow Wilson [24; 61].

Progressives applauded what Wilson had accomplished as president during his first year, but their agenda of social justice went well beyond even two such important measures as lowering the tariff and reforming the banking system. Reformers advocated assistance for organized labor, agricultural credits supported by the government for the farm sector, and legislation to curb child labor. To these more sweeping efforts to give the government a larger role in society, Wilson was less sympathetic. His reform impulse during his first term reflected the limitations of the Democratic party as far as a more powerful government was concerned. Any regulatory measures that might give legitimacy to government power over race relations in the South were intolerable to southern Democrats in Congress. Wilson still shared this point of view [24; 61].

REPUBLICAN REVIVAL AND PROGRESSIVE DECLINE

While Wilson and his administration had accomplished a great deal in their first year in office, there were indications that the tide of reform was slowing as 1914 began. The Progressive party that Theodore Roosevelt had established a year and a half earlier had not been able to create a viable organization that would keep it going toward major party status for the next presidential contest. Establishing a major party proved to be an expensive endeavor that demanded money, time, and enthusiasm, all of which ebbed away once the votes were counted in 1912. Roosevelt had displayed some sustained interest in his brainchild during the first half of 1913, but then he became distracted with other personal interests. He left for a trip to the Brazilian jungle late in 1913 in what he described as his last chance to be a boy again, and was out of the country until the following spring. His trip left him enfeebled from diseases, and even his prodigious energy was much depleted. Without his charismatic presence to inspire the party, the Progressive base began to crumble. The more conservative members drifted back toward the Republicans. The reformist elements in the party were restless and offered potential converts for Wilson and the Democrats [28].

Meanwhile, the Republicans experienced a general revival in their fortunes as the passions of 1912 eased. The progressives who had remained with the Republicans, such as La Follette and Irvine Lenroot of Wisconsin, Albert B. Cummins of Iowa, and a number of midwestern congressmen, discussed reorganizing the party to give the southern delegates less clout at the national convention. The power of the South within the Democratic party also acted to push the Republicans closer together. Sectional tensions between North and South, which had rested beneath the surface during the years of Republican dominance, reappeared and acted as a cohesive element for divergent Republicans [69].

In general, sentiment for reform also receded as 1914 began. After a decade of political agitation, voters were less enthusiastic about an activist government whose programs involved higher taxes and a larger bureaucracy. The onset of a recession during the spring of 1914 contributed to a feeling in the country at large that a lessening of reform initiatives might be in order. The Republicans capitalized on the signs of an economic downturn. In December James R. Mann, the House Republican leader, declared that 'the country is in the midst of a financial and industrial panic.' As 1914 unfolded and the economy stayed stagnant, Republicans spoke of 'the empty dinner pail' which they blamed on the Democratic tariff and the identification of Wilson's party with reform ideas. It looked to the Republicans as if 1914 might repeat their success of 1894 [69 *pp. 93, 102*].

CORPORATE REFORM

In this difficult political setting, Wilson and his party had to deal with the issue of corporate regulation, the third leg of the New Freedom. The president came at the question in a less aggressive posture toward the business community than he had advanced during the 1912 campaign. When he asked Congress to work on the issue in January 1914, he said that 'the antagonism between business and Government is over,' and that lawmaking would proceed on the assumption that the two sides could 'meet each other halfway in a common effort to square business methods with both public opinion and the law' [28 *p. 173*].

The process of regulating business practices first followed the broad outlines of the original New Freedom program. The measures embraced the Clayton Act which endeavored to state precisely what corporate activities were forbidden, an Interstate Trade Commission that looked to Theodore Roosevelt's Bureau of Corporations for its model, and a bill that would have empowered the Interstate Commerce Commission to oversee the bonds and stocks that railroads issued. Republicans complained that 'There is nothing in any of the Democratic antitrust bills that will build a fire that is not out, start a factory, or in any way encourage business' [69 *p. 100*].

Although Wilson had originally thought that a new, more specific anti-trust law would address the problem of illegal business practices, by the summer of 1914 he had changed his mind. Under the influence of Brandeis, he decided that a Trade Commission to supervise business on a continuing basis would be preferable. With Wilson's endorsement, Democrats passed both the Clayton Antitrust Act and the Federal Trade Commission in September 1914. In essence, the president had come back to the idea of a regulatory commission that Roosevelt had advanced in the 1912 campaign [24; 28].

By that time, the Wilson administration was sending signals that it thought the time for additional reforms had passed. As the business picture darkened during the first half of 1914, the president sought to conciliate business and reassure capitalists that the administration bore them no ill will. With the 1914 congressional elections in the offing, the White House went even further in the fall. The president told reporters that 'he had nearly reached the end of his economic program as outlined in the campaign and the Democratic platform' [28 *p. 173*].

These presidential indicators did not please the reform wing of Wilson's party nor the increasingly vocal interest groups that were advancing progressive causes in the years just before World War I. Wilson made it clear, however, to the advocates of woman suffrage, to the proponents of child labor legislation, and to those who wanted government encouragement of labor unions that his view of the reach of federal power was limited [24].

THE 1914 ELECTIONS AND BEYOND

As the summer of 1914 began, the stage seemed set for an election in which the Republicans would make sizeable gains in Congress, particularly in the House of Representatives, the Progressive party would recede, and the Democrats might repeat some of their problems of the 1890s. Further momentum for specific reforms also seemed problematic [24; 28; 69].

Then came the outbreak of World War I in August 1914, which gave progressivism in the United States a temporary reprieve before the essential conservatism of the nation reasserted itself. In the 1914 elections, the Democrats invoked the argument that Wilson could preserve neutrality better than the Republicans and limited their losses in that contest. The Republicans made gains in the House; the Democrats added seats in the Senate. More important, Wilson grasped that identifying his party with some of the reforms he had earlier scorned would win over former Progressives and help him in the South and West [24; 43].

During the next two years, the president pushed for child labor laws, woman suffrage, farm credits, and the eight-hour day for railroad workers. Coupled with his ability to maintain neutrality and a resurgence in the

American economy because of war orders, Wilson was able to run on a platform of peace, prosperity, and reform in 1916 and eke out a very narrow victory over his Republican rival, Charles Evans Hughes. It is a measure of the waning strength of reform that Wilson, with issues on his side and a weak candidate against him, regained the White House by such a tenuous margin [24; 28].

WAR AND THE CLIMAX OF REFORM

When the United States entered the war in April 1917, the resulting anti-German sentiments helped propel the adoption of prohibition as a war measure. The Anti-Saloon League and its allies advanced the notion that the grains used in alcoholic beverages could be put to better use in feeding European allies and the fighting men in the field. Propaganda against German influences in the United States further discredited the wet cause. By 1919 the Prohibition Amendment had been adopted and legislation to implement its principles soon followed. Despite the checkered history of prohibition during the 1920s, its place is secure as one of the significant manifestations of the reform spirit during the Progressive Era.

Woman suffrage advocates also promoted their reform as a means of offsetting 'alien' influence in elections while male soldiers were overseas. They obtained House approval for suffrage in 1918, and the Senate followed suit, with some reluctance, in 1919. Ratification of the suffrage amendment was completed in 1920. The achievement of suffrage did not transform the nature of American politics as feminists had hoped. The coalition that had pushed for suffrage soon disappeared. In the 1920s and later, women voted much as men did.

Immigration restriction gained backers as a way of avoiding a flood of newcomers once the fighting was ended. In the early years of the 1920s, restrictive legislation closed off entry into the United States to immigrants from Southern and Eastern Europe. Entry into the United States would remain difficult until reforms occurred in the mid-1960s.

By 1918, when the Republicans regained control of Congress, most of the basic spirit of progressive reform had vanished. The voters wanted lower taxes, smaller government, less bureaucracy, fewer regulations – what Warren G. Harding summed up during the 1920 election campaign in the word 'Normalcy.' A generation of reform had exhausted the electorate and allowed the natural conservatism of American voters to resurface.

For the major actors in the political drama over progressivism and reform, the years after 1914 brought disappointment or tragedy. Theodore Roosevelt became a staunch opponent of Wilson's foreign policy during the period of American neutrality, but his advocacy of pro-Allied policies alienated many in the isolationist wing of the Republican party. Although

Roosevelt very much wanted to be the candidate of the Republicans in 1916, the party turned instead to Charles Evans Hughes. Roosevelt supported Hughes grudgingly, and was not surprised when the Republicans lost. The defeat added to Roosevelt's bitterness against the president.

When war came, Roosevelt wanted to raise a volunteer division to take to France as a symbol of American support for the Allied cause. President Wilson and the military blocked that initiative, and Roosevelt had to remain at home as an advocate of a tough peace settlement with Germany. Although he never lost the progressive impulses that he had demonstrated up to 1912, Roosevelt became a strident exponent of American nationalism through the election of 1918. He died a few months later on 6 January 1919. He had made a significant contribution to the strengthening of the presidential office during the first decade of the century and his ill-fated campaign in 1912 had set the agenda for American politics for decades to come.

His bitter enemy, Woodrow Wilson, also experienced the shifts of political fortune after winning a second term in 1916. Once the nation was embroiled in World War I, Wilson ran the conflict on a partisan basis, and gave Republicans little opportunity to participate in a meaningful manner. As a result, rancor between the president and the opposition grew in intensity. Despite a personal plea from the president himself, the voters turned against Wilson in 1918 and returned the Republicans to control of Congress.

The Paris Peace Conference of 1919 created the League of Nations, an international organization that aimed to prevent future war, and Wilson supported this initiative enthusiastically. Unfortunately, the Senate, led by Roosevelt's friend Henry Cabot Lodge, rejected the Treaty of Versailles with the League at its core, and the United States stayed aloof from a direct connection with European affairs. Wilson suffered a crippling stroke in 1919, and left office in 1921 a broken and defeated man. He died three years later in 1924.

As president, however, Wilson had made the Democrats the party of governmental activism and regulation to an extent that would have seemed unthinkable during the era of Grover Cleveland. The dependence of the Democrats on the South meant that there were still limits on how far the party would accept regulation as a policy, but Wilson had moved them in a direction that anticipated the New Deal coalition of Franklin D. Roosevelt. He had also shown what a strong president could do as a legislative leader with a sympathetic party and a coherent agenda. With two progressive presidents in Roosevelt and Wilson, reform received a legitimacy that it would not have obtained if it had been associated with only one of the two major parties.

William Howard Taft became more popular as a former president than he had ever been in the White House, and he attained his life's ambition when President Warren G. Harding named him as Chief Justice of the United States in 1921. Taft's Court proved very conservative as it overturned some of the key achievements of progressive reform such as the child labor law that had finally passed in 1916. Taft died in 1930.

For Senator Robert M. La Follette, the White House remained a persistent but elusive goal. His opposition to the World War made him a derided figure in the Senate as long as hostilities continued, but he rebounded in the wake of disillusion with the conflict. He ran as an independent candidate for president in 1924 but came in third behind Calvin Coolidge and John W. Davis. La Follette died a year later.

Progressivism and its spirit seemed dead as the 1920s began. Warren G. Harding and Calvin Coolidge were very different presidents from Roosevelt and Wilson, and the sense that government could be used for broad social purposes became anachronistic in the capitalistic heyday of the 1920s. The pre-war reformers drifted into other professions or waited for the political wheel to turn once again. When the Depression of the 1930s came and with it the New Deal of Franklin D. Roosevelt, many of the old Progressives found the activist government of the 1930s to be a repudiation of what they had stood for.

Progressivism and its adherents had, however, made a positive difference in American history. Politics was a less corrupt and more open process by 1914 than it had been a generation earlier. Americans took less interest in public affairs, but that change owed something to the rise of mass entertainment and greater leisure. The place of the political party had been much reduced and in its stead had come the government agency. There was still a confidence that disinterested, non-partisan experts could manage the nation's affairs in a more efficient manner than politicians had done. Progressives were confident that regulation offered a preferable path to social justice than either *laissez-faire* capitalism òr government ownership.

In the process, real social inequities had been addressed. Workers had more legal protections by 1914 than would have seemed possible twenty-five years earlier. Child labor remained a blot on society, but its incidence had been somewhat reduced. Labor unions, while not yet strong, had a legitimacy and standing that the 1890s had denied to the laboring classes. The conviction that progress lay in reducing social injustice, not in increasing it, was one of the significant legacies of the age of reform.

Not all problems had been solved, to be sure. The blight of racism had been largely outside the progressive agenda. In the South lynching continued and segregation was entrenched. Unhappy African Americans had begun to move north after 1913 in what became known as the 'Great Migration.' Their presence in the great cities of the Northeast and Middle West made racial prejudice a national issue for the century ahead. The Progressive Era had laid the tentative beginnings for effective black protest in the rise of the National Association for the Advancement of Colored People and the protests against segregation in Washington and elsewhere. These developments had occurred not because of the spirit of reform, but in spite of it.

If they had not resolved all of the questions that faced their nation, Americans between 1890 and 1914 had identified the problems and proposed answers that set the terms of debate down to the end of the twentieth century. In the year 2000, politicians still argued about whether the reforms of the Progressive Era were worth keeping. Some were dispensed with, as occurred in the dismantling of the Interstate Commerce Commission. Some conservative Republicans asserted that the increased power of the government at the beginning of the century had made the social problems of the 1990s inevitable. These questions were for a future generation of Americans to ponder. The citizens who lived through the twenty-five years from the Billion Dollar Congress to the Guns of August 1914 had set the social priorities for a century and proposed answers whose resonance remained strong. In 1974 a historian said that the progressives had been one of the great constructive forces in the nation's history, trailing only the Founding Fathers and the architects of the New Deal [27 *p. 200*]. As the United States observes the centennial of the Progressive Era, that judgment seems more securely grounded and likely to endure as a thoughtful summing up of an age and the people who made it.

PART THREE DOCUMENTS

On 4 July 1892 the People's Party met in Omaha, Nebraska. The preamble to their platform, written by long-time protestor Ignatius Donnelly of Minnesota, invoked the spirit of the agrarian protest that animated American politics for the next four years.

The conditions which surround us best justify our cooperation: we meet in the midst of a nation brought to the verge of moral, political, and material ruin. Corruption dominates the ballot-box, the legislatures, the Congress, and touches even the ermine of the bench. The people are demoralized; most of the States have been compelled to isolate the voters at the polling-places to prevent universal intimidation or bribery. The newspapers are largely subsidized or muzzled; public opinion silenced; business prostrated; our homes covered with mortgages; labor impoverished; and the land concentrating in the hands of the capitalists. The urban workmen are denied the right of organization for self-protection; imported pauperized labor beats down their wages; a hireling standing army, unrecognized by our laws, is established to shoot them down, and they are rapidly degenerating into European conditions. The fruits of the toil of millions are boldly stolen to build up colossal fortunes for a few, unprecedented in the history of mankind; and the possessors of these, in turn, despise the republic and endanger liberty. From the same prolific womb of governmental injustice we breed the two great classes – tramps and millionaires.

John D. Hicks, *The Populist Revolt: A History of the Farmers' Alliance and People's Party* (Minneapolis, Minnesota: University of Minnesota Press, 1931; reprinted by University of Nebraska Press, 1961), pp. 439–40.

DOCUMENT 2   BRYAN AND THE CROSS OF GOLD

In 1896 William Jennings Bryan became nationally prominent when he delivered the 'Cross of Gold' speech at the Democratic National Convention in Chicago. Bryan's remarks reflect the tension between country and city that lay behind the debate over the proper kind of metal on which the American currency should be based. Bryan was a champion of the inflationary doctrine of free silver. His remarks also respond to the criticism that unilateral American action to make silver coinage legal would result in financial losses at the hands of other nations, especially Great Britain.

You come to us and tell us that the great cities are in favor of the gold standard; we reply that the great cities rest upon our broad and fertile prairies. Burn down your cities and leave our farms, and your cities will spring up again as if by magic; but destroy our farms and the grass will grow in the streets of every city in the country.

My friends, we declare that this nation is able to legislate for its own people on every question, without waiting for the aid or consent of any other nation on earth; and upon that issue we expect to carry every state in the Union. I shall not slander the inhabitants of the fair state of Massachusetts nor the inhabitants of the state of New York by saying that, when they are confronted with the proposition, they will declare that this nation is not able to attend to its own business. It is the issue of 1776 over again. Our ancestors, when but three million in number, had the courage to declare their political independence of every other nation; shall we, their descendants, when we have grown to seventy millions, declare that we are less independent than our forefathers?

No, my friends, that will never be the verdict of our people. Therefore, we care not upon what lines the battle is fought. If they say bimetallism is good, but that we cannot have it until other nations help us, we reply, that instead of having a gold standard because England has, we will restore bimetallism, and then let England have bimetallism because the United States has it. If they dare to come out in the open field and defend the gold standard as a good thing, we will fight them to the uttermost. Having behind us the producing masses of the nation and the world, supported by the commercial interests, the laboring interests, and the toilers everywhere, we will answer their demand for a gold standard by saying to them: You shall not press down upon the brow of labor this crown of thorns, you shall not crucify mankind upon a cross of gold.

Henry Steele Commager, ed., *Documents of American History*, 2 vols (Englewood Cliffs, New Jersey: Prentice Hall, 1988), vol. I, pp. 627–8.

DOCUMENT 3   **SEPARATE BUT EQUAL IN RACIAL MATTERS:**
             PLESSY v. *FERGUSON*, 1896

By the end of the nineteenth century, the United States was a society where racial segregation governed life throughout the South. In 1896 the Supreme Court ruled in the case of Plessy v. Ferguson *that the doctrine of separate but equal was constitutional. The case involved a Louisiana law specifying separate railroad cars for white and black. The doctrine enunciated by Justice Henry Billings Brown in the majority opinion remained in force until the 1950s and 1960s.*

We consider the underlying fallacy of the plaintiff's argument to consist in the assumption that the enforced separation of the two races stamps the colored race with a badge of inferiority. If this be so, it is not by reason of anything found in the act, but solely because the colored race chooses to put that construction upon it. The argument necessarily assumes that if, as has been more than once the case, and is not unlikely to be so again, the colored race should become the dominant power in the state legislature and should enact a law in precisely similar terms, it would thereby relegate the white race to an inferior position. We imagine that the white race, at least, would not acquiesce in this assumption. The argument also assumes that social prejudice may be overcome by legislation, and that equal rights cannot be secured to the Negro except by an enforced commingling of the two races. We cannot accept this proposition. If the two races are to meet on terms of social equality, it must be the result of natural affinities, a mutual appreciation of each other's merits and a voluntary consent of individuals ... Legislation is powerless to eradicate racial instincts or to abolish distinctions based upon physical differences, and the attempt to do so can only result in accentuating the difficulties of the present situation. If the civil and political right of both races be equal, one cannot be inferior to the other civilly or politically. If one race be inferior to the other socially, the Constitution of the United States cannot put them on the same plane.

Henry Steel Commager, *Documents of American History*, 2 vols (Englewood Cliffs, New Jersey: Prentice Hall, 1988), vol.I, p. 629.

DOCUMENT 4   **CARL SCHURZ ATTACKS IMPERIALISM**

Following the war with Spain, the issue of acquiring the Philippines became a source of major controversy. Anti-imperialists such as the noted German-American leader Carl Schurz argued that the United States was making a great mistake in pursuing an imperialist policy. In a speech at the University of Chicago on 4 January 1899, Schurz outlined some of his objections in the excerpts from his speech that are printed here.

Looking them in the face, let us clear our minds of confused notions about our duties and responsibilities in the premises. That our victories have devolved upon us certain duties as to the peoples of the conquered islands, I readily admit. But are they the only duties we have to perform, or have they suddenly become paramount to all other duties? I deny it. I deny that our duties we owe to the Cubans and the Porto Ricans, and the Filipinos, and the Tagals of the Asiatic islands absolve us from the duties to the seventy-five millions of our own people, and to their posterity. I deny that they oblige us to destroy the moral credit of our own republic by turning this loudly heralded war of liberation and humanity into a land-grabbing game and an act of criminal aggression. I deny that they compel us to aggravate our race troubles, to bring upon us the constant danger of war, and to subject our people to the galling burden of increasing armaments. If we have rescued those unfortunate daughters of Spain, the colonies, from the tyranny of their cruel father, I deny that we are therefore in honor bound to marry any of the girls, or to take them all into our household, where they may disturb and demoralize our whole family. I deny that the liberation of those Spanish dependencies morally constrains us to do anything that would put our highest mission to solve the great problem of democratic government in jeopardy, or that would otherwise endanger the vital interests of the republic. Whatever our duties to them may be, our duties to our own country and people stand first; and from this standpoint we have, as sane men and patriotic citizens, to regard our obligation to take care of the future of those islands and their people.

They fought for deliverance from Spanish oppression and we helped them to obtain that deliverance. That deliverance they understood to mean independence. I repeat the question whether anybody can tell me why the declaration of Congress that the Cubans *of right ought to be* free and independent should not apply to all of them? Their independence, therefore, would be the natural and rightful outcome. This is the solution of the problem first to be taken in view.

It is objected that they are not capable of independent government. They may answer that this is their affair and that they are at least entitled to a trial. I frankly admit that, if they are given that trial, their conduct in governing themselves will be far from perfect. Well, the conduct of no people is perfect, not even our own. They may try to revenge themselves upon their tories in their Revolutionary War. But we, too, threw our tories into hideous dungeons during our Revolutionary War, and persecuted and drove them away after its close. They may have bloody civil broils. But we, too, have had our Civil War which cost hundreds and thousands of lives and devastated one-half of our land; and now we have in horrible abundance the killings by lynch laws, and our battles at Virden. They may have trouble with their wild tribes. So had we, and we treated our wild tribes in a manner not to be proud of. They may have corruption and rapacity in their government, but Havana and Ponce may get municipal administration almost as good as New York has under Tammany rule; and Manila may secure a city council not much less virtuous than that of Chicago.

Carl Schurz, *American Imperialism: The Convocation Address Delivered on the Occasion of the Twenty-Seventh Convocation of the University of Chicago, Jan. 4, 1899* (Boston, Massachusetts: Dana Estes and Company, 1899), pp. 30–2.

PRESIDENT MCKINLEY ARGUES
FOR IMPERIALISM

Following the approval of the Treaty of Paris that ended the war with
Spain, President William McKinley traveled to Boston to address the Home
Market Club on 16 February 1899. The concluding passages of his remarks
capture well the position of the advocates of expansion toward the
Philippine Islands and the new role of the United States. Just ten days
earlier fighting had broken out between the Filipinos and the American
forces. The bracketed material about the audience response is in the original.

The future of the Philippine Islands is now in the hands of the American
people. [Applause] Until the treaty was ratified or rejected, the Executive
Department of this government could only preserve the peace and protect
life and property. That treaty now commits the free and enfranchised
Filipinos to the guiding hand and the liberalizing influences, the generous
sympathies, the uplifting education, not of their American masters, of their
American emancipators. [Great applause] No one can tell to-day what is
best for them or for us. I know no one at this hour who is wise enough or
sufficiently well informed to determine what form of government will best
subserve their interests and our interests, their and our well-being.

If we knew everything by intuition – and I sometimes think that there are
those who believe that if we do not they do [laughter and applause] – we
should not need information; but, unfortunately, most of us are not in that
happy state. This whole subject is now with Congress; and Congress is the
voice, the conscience, and the judgment of the American people. Upon their
judgment and conscience can we not rely? I believe in them. I trust them. I
know of no better or safer human tribunal than the people. [Great applause]

Until Congress shall direct otherwise, it will be the duty of the Executive
to possess and hold the Philippines, giving to the people thereof peace and
order and beneficent government; affording them every opportunity to
prosecute their lawful pursuits; encouraging them in thrift and industry;
making them feel and know that we are their friends, not their enemies,
that their good is our aim, that their welfare is our welfare, but that neither
their aspirations nor ours can be realized until our authority is acknow-
ledged and unquestioned. [Loud and enthusiastic applause]

That the inhabitants of the Philippines will be benefited by this republic
is my unshaken belief. That they will have a kindlier government under our
guidance, and that they will be aided in every possible way to be a self-

respecting and self-governing people, is as true as that the American people love liberty and have an abiding faith in their own government and in their own institutions. [Great applause] No imperial designs lurk in the American mind. They are alien to American sentiment, thought, and purpose. Our priceless principles undergo no change under a tropic sun. They go with the flag. [Long-continued applause]

> Why read ye not the changeless truth
> The free can conquer but to save? [Great applause]

If we can benefit these remote peoples, who will object? If, in the years of the future, they are established in government under law and liberty, who will regret our perils and sacrifices? Who will not rejoice in our heroism and humanity? Always perils, and always after them safety; always darkness and clouds, but always shining through them the light and sunshine; always cost and sacrifice, but always after them the fruition of liberty, education, and civilization. [Enthusiastic applause]

I have no light or knowledge not common to my countrymen. I do not prophesy. The present is all-absorbing to me. But I cannot bound my vision by the blood-stained trenches around Manila – where every red drop, whether from the veins of an American soldier or a misguided Filipino, is anguish to my heart – but by the broad range of future years, when that group of islands, under the impulse of the year just past, shall have become the gems and glories of those tropical seas – a land of plenty and of increasing possibilities; a people redeemed from savage indolence and habits, devoted to the arts of peace, in touch with the commerce and trade of all nations, enjoying the blessings of freedom, of civil and religious liberty, of education, and of homes, and whose children and children's children shall for ages hence bless the American republic because it emancipated and redeemed their fatherland, and set them in the pathway of the world's best civilization. [Prolonged applause]

Speeches and Addresses of William McKinley From March 1, 1897 to May 30, 1900 (New York, New York: Doubleday & McClure, 1900), pp. 191–3.

DOCUMENT 6   **A CRITIQUE OF THE PROTECTIVE TARIFF BY A REPUBLICAN**

The tariff issue had become the primary economic doctrine of the Republicans in the 1890s. A decade later it had emerged as a political liability. James R. Garfield, who later followed Theodore Roosevelt into the Progressive party, wrote to the president in 1902 to express his unhappiness with the protective tariff policy. Roosevelt took no action on the letter, but

Garfield's ideas would become common among Republican reformers as the decade progressed.

The purpose of the protective policy was primarily to develop our home industries and supply our home market. This has been splendidly well done. The next step was to develop our foreign trade. This was done as soon as our home industries were strong enough to compete with the world, and in this competition protection is not necessary to the extent originally granted. The great mass of our people look at this question from a purely practical standpoint. They have no inclination to destroy, or even impede, industrial progress, but they properly demand that the American consumer of American products be given as good prices as the foreign consumer of American products.

Tariff modification, like trust regulation, is an economic necessity. It will not down any easier than Banquo's ghost, and the political party that attempts to avoid or shirk the issue will meet and merit disaster. I do not urge a general tariff revision, and think unwise any movement which would be construed as an assault on the general policy of a protective tariff; but the announcement of our willingness to undertake a rational, businesslike modification of rates which are proved too high would show the people of the country that the Republican party is still the party of rational progress.

The tree of protection, to whose spreading branches our Republican orators point with just pride, has grown a little straggly in places – has some dead limbs, some excrescences. In fact it needs pruning; and I would rather keep it in the care of a Republican forester who knows and appreciates its value than turn it over to the hostile ax of a Democrat who would try to destroy it root and branch.

James R. Garfield to Theodore Roosevelt, 17 September 1902, James R. Garfield Papers,
Manuscripts Division, Library of Congress, Washington, DC.

DOCUMENT 7   PROHIBITION AND REFORM

The issue of alcohol control was one that divided progressives. Many reformers believed that the liquor traffic was a sinister special interest like the railroads or the oil companies. Other progressives thought that the state should stay out of personal behavior. In this excerpt, Dr John Marshall Barker of Boston University states the case for regulating the saloon as a goal that progressives could share.

The moral aspects of the drink habit may no longer be considered an open question. History and religion accord with the verdict of civilized society to-day, – that the drink habit is an evil to be shunned by all who regard personal worth and social welfare. The leading Christian churches enjoin upon their members total abstinence as a moral duty, and urge the legal prohibition of intoxicants as a beverage. Undoubtedly the beverage-drink traffic is a complex social problem with many ramifications. The paramount issue is whether or not the individual shall project into the realm of society his personal privilege in the use of intoxicants by opening up a saloon to traffic in vice and make it institutional in character; and, further, whether or not this same saloon-keeper, with the view of extending and protecting the traffic, has the right to join with other saloon-keepers and form a strong, compact organization which shall seek to control legislation, intimidate executive officers, and by its united political and financial influence threaten the peace and sanctity of the home and defeat the suffrage rights of the people. It is plain that the definite issue that confronts us is not whether the individual shall use intoxicating liquors as a beverage, but whether the saloon as a social menace shall be maintained or suppressed.

No one should be diverted or side-tracked by fixing his attention upon the irrelevant question of sumptuary legislation [regulating behavior], personal liberty, or the probable value of the beverage use of alcoholic liquors. The all-important question centres about the saloon. All lovers of sobriety and social order may agree upon this point of view. By standing upon this common ground they may bring all the beneficent social forces into union for a strenuous and vehement crusade against the saloon as the enemy of social well-being and progress.

John Marshall Barker, *The Saloon Problem and the Social Problem* (Boston, Massachusetts: Everett Press, 1905), pp. 1–2.

DOCUMENT 8	A CONSERVATIVE OPPOSES RAILROAD REGULATION

As Theodore Roosevelt's campaign for railroad regulation and government supervision of railroad rates gathered momentum in 1906, conservatives became increasingly unhappy with the direction in which the president was leading the country. This letter from a prominent railroad president to a leading Republican senator captures the spirit of these complaints.

I do not believe any question more important to the country than this Rate question was ever before you, because Government rate making means pretty soon Government ownership and the political as well as commercial consequences must to say the least be serious. It is not a Railroad question. Transportation by Rail is either 'business' or it is not. That is the question. It cannot for long be both 'business' and 'not business;' it must be one or the other. If not business it is politics, and if so decided by the Senate the man on horseback will soon come to stay. We do not know perhaps what the commercial consequences of Government rate making may be, but we can see, it seems to me, what the political consequences *must* be. Both will undoubtedly be bad enough.

I sometimes wonder if the current which carries us along may not bring us up against practical socialism ending in some kind of a revolution before so very long – not in our day but soon. Or will the common sense of the people get tired of the actors and charlatans who are now in the saddle, and return to sound first principles? Does the current of human affairs admit of that. How much depends, in this country, on the Senate, and yet the people do not appreciate it.

Charles E. Perkins to Senator William Boyd Allison, 26 February 1906, William Boyd Allison Papers, Iowa State Department of History and Archives, Des Moines, Iowa, Box 359.

DOCUMENT 9	A REPUBLICAN SUPPORTS RAILROAD REGULATION

While conservative Republican businessmen attacked railroad regulation, other party members endorsed the new policy. James S. Clarkson was a Republican official in New York City who had long been active in politics in his native Iowa. He wrote to Senator Jonathan P. Dolliver of Iowa in March 1906 to praise Dolliver's leadership in the battle in the Senate over what would become the Hepburn Act.

You have lifted the conflict up and put it on the high plane of human interest and human duty, and while you have given the men who are drawing fifty and a hundred thousand dollars salary for mismanaging the great corporations plain notice of what will come if they do not understand the will of the people as shown at present, you have given the warning in a manner of which they cannot complain. There is no doubt that the railway corporations themselves need this kind of a law for protection, and the complaints do not come from the railway corporations, but from the men who are officers of them at high salaries and, beyond that, in collusion with the big trusts and monopolies sharing in personal profits at the expense of the property they are pretending to serve. Some people I have talked to today, coming in from the West, say that you are getting hold of the hearts of all the people out there and that such strong papers as the Chicago Tribune are giving you proper recognition. I am glad, but not surprised, to hear this. It is strange that the corporation managers are so blind that they do not see that the people have started in to accomplish this legislation and that it cannot be outwitted, thwarted, side-tracked or defeated. They hate

Roosevelt because he insists on this legislation, but they ought to understand that he will be President until it is accomplished; or, if he is not, some
other men as much beyond their reach through fear or purchase will take
his place and accomplish what he started out to achieve.

James S. Clarkson to Jonathan P. Dolliver, 6 March 1906, Jonathan P. Dolliver Papers, Iowa
Historical Society, Iowa City, Iowa.

DOCUMENT 10   **A SOUTHERN PROGRESSIVE ADVOCATES
RESTRICTIONS ON UNIVERSAL SUFFRAGE**

*In the South progressive ideas often expressed themselves as opposition to
participation by African Americans in the politics of the Democratic party
and elections generally. One of the leaders of such a movement was a Texan
named Alexander Watkins Terrell (1827–1912), who authored election
laws making it more difficult for blacks to vote in the state. In March 1906
Terrell spoke before the National Civic Federation in New York City, and
his views about who should be allowed to vote expressed those of many
'reformers' in the South in this period. In his discussion of election laws, he
refers to the laws of other southern states that allowed men to vote who
were literate and could show an 'understanding' of the Constitution. That
device was used to exclude blacks in a state such as Mississippi.*

What the country now needs, both North and South, is a system of election
laws which will tend to diminish the depraved, the purchasable, and the
reckless class of voters, and to increase the power of the patriotic, the
interested and the thoughtful class of citizens. We in Texas regard an educational test as dangerous and have faith that we can get along until we can
educate all our people. If a man must be able to write and to read the
Federal Constitution and understand it before he can vote, the standard is
under a strict examination, too high, for even statesmen have differed for
over a century about the meaning of the Constitution, and the prejudices of
a partisan election judge would often exclude a worthy voter. And yet any
system based on the desire to have what is called a full vote must end in
failure. What the country needs is a *voluntary* and honest vote and not a
full vote that is controlled at the polls by the ward heeler [an operative of
the urban machine], the campaign boss, or the machine demagogue. Whether
universal manhood suffrage is good for the country depends entirely on the
sort of men who vote. Universal suffrage exercised under machine methods,
and by those who are depraved and ignorant of national or State policies,
means a dangerous oligarchy, for leaders will control the vote. True the
machine that triumphs may be changed by the same dangerous vote, but the

change is only to another oligarchy. In the experiment of free government this seems disheartening, but our experience thus far encourages us to hope that the greatest good for the greatest number will finally be secured in the future under our representative system.

Good election laws are of slow growth; they must be evolved by experience, and the expedients of corrupt men to circumvent them must be met by new remedies. In the absence of universal intelligence the only safeguard for a permanent democracy will be found in restricting suffrage to those who in *some way* show an honest interest in public affairs.

Speech on Elections, 1906, Alexander Watkins Terrell Papers, Center for American History, University of Texas at Austin, Austin, Texas.

DOCUMENT 11   WOMEN'S CLUBS ATTACK CHILD LABOR

The reform spirit owed much to the organizing and lobbying efforts of women who endorsed specific legislative goals. One of the most persistent campaigns was the effort to curb child labor abuses in both North and South. Women's groups sent petitions to the Congress asking for legislation to address the problem. In this document the Michigan State Federation of Women's Clubs makes its case to its Senator, Julius Caesar Burrows, a conservative Republican.

The industrial situation before us today demanding the most earnest attention of club women is that of Child Labor. There is a pronounced increase of Child Labor, not alone in the cotton industries of the South, but in the textile mills of the northern and middle states; and where legislation has been enacted to correct and nullify this evil, enforcement has been found most defective. 'There is need of a vigorous and imperative public sentiment in favor of the enforcement of the laws, for without the pressure of public sentiment, the best laws remain dead letters.'

It is authoritatively stated that this piteous army of child labors is steadily increasing and now numbers 2,000,000. The children are hurried from the cradle into the factories, with no childhood, no sweet memories of playtime or of home, nothing for them but toil from morning until night, and only fifteen minutes in which to eat a cold lunch; their frail bodies are often twisted and misshapen, the intellect obscured, the will paralyzed. These little white slaves of the 20th century are mostly American children. In this free land they are toiling under the glorious flag of liberty to satisfy the greed of commercialism.

Your committee, therefore, recommends the study of Child Labor, as a means to an end, in the abolishment of this national evil; that standing committees be appointed; that one or more programs on the study of Child Labor be presented, and that local conditions be investigated and reported to the Chairman of this committee.

Juliet S. Goodenow, Chairman Industrial Committee, Michigan State Federation of Women's Clubs, to Julius Caesar Burrows, 16 March 1906, in National Archives, *Our Mothers Before Us: Women and Democracy 1789–1920* (Washington, DC: Foundation for the National Archives, 1998), Section V, p. 36.

DOCUMENT 12   **THEODORE ROOSEVELT ON MUCKRAKING JOURNALISM**

In April 1906 Theodore Roosevelt spoke out against what came to be known as the muckrakers. Roosevelt borrowed an image from John Bunyan's Pilgrim's Progress, *and the label stuck. In the president's mind the crusading journalist had attacked honest men, some of them in the United States Senate where Roosevelt needed votes for his regulatory program – hence the attack on the journalists and writers whom he had previously supported. The muckrakers never really recovered from Roosevelt's assault.*

In Bunyan's 'Pilgrim's Progress' you may recall the description of the Man with the Muck-rake, the man who could look no way but downward, with the muckrake in his hand; who was offered a celestial crown for his muck-rake, but who would neither look up nor regard the crown he was offered, but continued to rake to himself the filth of the floor.

In 'Pilgrim's Progress' the Man with the Muck-rake is set forth as the example of him whose vision is fixed on carnal instead of spiritual things. Yet he also typifies the man who in this life consistently refuses to see aught that is lofty, and fixes his eyes with solemn intentness only on that which is vile and debasing. Now, it is very necessary that we should not flinch from seeing what is vile and debasing. There is filth on the floor, and it must be scraped up with the muck-rake; and there are times and places where this service is most needed of all the services that can be performed. But the man who never does anything else, who never thinks or speaks or writes, save of his feats with the muck-rake, speedily becomes, not a help to society, not an incitement to good, but one of the most potent forces for evil.

There are, in the body politic, economic and social, many and grave evils, and there is urgent necessity for the sternest war upon them. There should be relentless exposure of and attack upon every evil man whether politician or business man, every evil practice, whether in politics, in business, or in social life. I hail as a benefactor every writer or speaker, every man who, on the platform, or in book, magazine, or newspaper, with merciless severity makes such attack, provided always that he in his turn remembers that the attack is of use only if it is absolutely truthful. The liar is no whit better than the thief, and if his mendacity takes the form of slander, he may be worse than most thieves. It puts a premium upon knavery untruthfully to attack an honest man, or even with hysterical exaggeration to assail a bad man with untruth. An epidemic of indiscriminate assault upon character does not good, but very great harm. The soul of every scoundrel is gladdened whenever an honest man is assailed, or even when a scoundrel is untruthfully assailed.

'The Man With the Muck-rake,' Speech of 14 April 1906, Theodore Roosevelt, *The Works of Theodore Roosevelt. Vol. XVI: American Problems* (New York, New York: Charles Scribner's Sons, 1926), pp. 415–16.

DOCUMENT 13   AN ASSESSMENT OF THEODORE ROOSEVELT'S PRESIDENCY, 1909

When Roosevelt's presidency came to an end in March 1909, newspapers and magazines surveyed his administration to measure the effects of his years in the White House. An excerpt from an editorial in the religious weekly The Independent *captures well how Roosevelt's performance looked to observers at the time.*

And this brings us to his career as President. The notable thing about his two Presidential terms is the multitude of things he has said and done, not in the ordinary routine of official service, but from the initiative of his own brain. He has let nothing drift. He has waited for no occasion to force his hand. He has been on the masthead looking for foes to fight or friends to help. The world has come to look on him as its mentor and leader. Who but he would have uttered the world's voice that the war between Russia and Japan must end, and summoned the combatants to parley for peace at Portsmouth? Who but he, a rich man's son, dared to tackle the combinations of wealth, and compelled them to cease their unfair competition with their weaker competitors? That has been a long hard fight, and Theodore Roosevelt has been the principal champion in it, himself the leader of both parties and most opposed in his own. He has demanded a square deal, and we have loved him for the enemies he has made. It would have been vastly easier to keep quiet, and let natural selection and the laws of trade work their prettiest and their worst, but he wanted the just thing done, and done by law, and he deserves the credit.

These labors of war and peace and business have had many ramifications, in which he has had to originate and direct, but they have not been enough to exhaust his energy. He has taught us to honor the strenuous life. He has emphasized domestic duty and the evil of race suicide, and his has been the example of the head of a pure, simple, faithful and fruitful home. He has purified the civil service of the nation as well as its business methods and its domestic life by example and precept and rule, and the whole country is better for what he has done; and even railroads and corporations confess that what he has compelled them to do has been for their good also.

He has protected our forests, urged a simple life, ended a mischievous conflict with coal-miners, investigated agricultural conditions, and swiftly turned, as the chance came to foreign interests, Hague Conference, open door in Manchuria, opium suppression, Central American federation, naval enlargement, Panama Canal, South American good will, and a hundred other matters we cannot take space to mention, until he has made himself the dominant forceful factor in both continents.

He has been persistent as well as strenuous, has written more messages and made more addresses, and traveled more miles than any other President, and talked more sermons on honesty and faithfulness until not a few were tired of them; but the good common people have accepted them and believed in him as their spokesman for whatever is fair and square and right.

'Theodore Roosevelt,' *The Independent*, 66 (4 March 1909): 491–2.

DOCUMENT 14   A FRIEND DEFENDS PRESIDENT TAFT'S RECORD

By the summer of 1910 the tension between Taft and Roosevelt over the future of the Republican party had intensified. Roosevelt's return from his African trip did not smooth over the rift. One of Taft's close friends, Mabel Boardman, wrote a letter defending the president to a Republican congressman from Kansas named Victor Murdock. A portion of her argument is given here.

I cannot help feeling and I think you will agree with me in this that so far the President has not received a 'square deal' from his predecessor. Whatever Col. Roosevelt may think of the tariff, this was not one of his policies. He never even in one of his many messages that I can recall ventured to discuss a matter known to be of all the problems the most difficult for a president to undertake with popular success. Therefore as far as the tariff is concerned it has had absolutely nothing to do with the carrying out of his policies.

As for his other policies, those for conservation, railroad rate regulation, methods leading to the control of corporations, etc. the President has with the aid of Congress carried forward these policies through legislation into law. Carrying out the promises of the Republican platform and of his own inaugural address to enforce these policies by the enactment of law the

President merits the approval and support of all Republicans. In all of Col. Roosevelt's seven years no such amount of legislation was passed. You know how much of this progressive legislation was against the inclinations of a certain old element in both House and Senate and how hard the President had to labor with this element to carry it through. The public, because of the President's natural modesty, does not know and may never know his share in all this work. You remember the old story of the wind, the sun and the traveller with his cloak, how the quiet persistence of the sun won over the roistering efforts of the wind. So has the President worked for the sake of the public good.

Having done all this, having for twenty years been a most loyal, true and faithful friend of Col. Roosevelts, serving under him with absolute fidelity, adding to the success of his administrations by *his* remarkable success in dealing with the complex problems of Cuba and the Philippines and by his work in the cabinet, is it not strange that since the latter's [Roosevelt's] return so far not one single word of commendation of President Taft has he uttered in public. It would seem as if the success of the President was a source of annoyance rather than a satisfaction to him.

Mabel Boardman to Victor Murdock, 24 August 1910, Papers of Mabel Boardman, Box 5, Manuscript Division, Library of Congress.

DOCUMENT 15 THEODORE ROOSEVELT CALLS FOR THE NEW NATIONALISM

On 31 August 1910 in a speech at Osawatomie, Kansas, Theodore Roosevelt articulated his doctrine of regulatory activism that became known as the New Nationalism. In this speech, Roosevelt went beyond the Square Deal of his presidency and looked forward to the later reforms of the twentieth century.

I do not ask for overcentralization; but I do ask that we work in a spirit of broad and far-reaching nationalism when we work for what concerns our people as a whole. We are all Americans. Our common interests are as broad as the continent. I speak to you here in Kansas exactly as I would speak in New York or Georgia, for the most vital problems are those which affect us alike. The National Government belongs to the whole American people, and where the whole American people are interested, that interest can be guarded effectively only by the National Government. The betterment which we seek must be accomplished, I believe, mainly through the National Government.

The American people are right in demanding that New Nationalism, without which we cannot hope to deal with new problems. The New

Nationalism puts the national need before sectional or personal advantage. It is impatient of the utter confusion that results from local legislatures attempting to treat national issues as local issues. It is still more impatient of the impotence which springs from overdivision of governmental powers, the impotence which makes it possible for local selfishness or legal cunning hired by wealthy special interests to bring national activities to a deadlock. This New Nationalism regards the executive power as the steward of the public welfare. It demands of the judiciary that it shall be interested primarily in human welfare rather than in property, just as it demands that the representative body shall represent all the people rather than any one class or section of the people.

Theodore Roosevelt, *The Works of Theodore Roosevelt. Vol. XVII: Social Justice and Popular Rule* (New York, New York: Charles Scribner's Sons, 1926), pp. 19–20.

DOCUMENT 16 A PROGRESSIVE INDICTMENT OF POLITICAL PARTIES

By 1910 the sentiment against political parties had persuaded some progressives of the need for non-partisan action as a way of influencing the Republican party in the direction of greater change. In this letter, Frederic C. Howe, a reform writer, presents his plan for such a program to Senator Robert M. La Follette of Wisconsin.

And I have been thinking of a movement to promote legislation in the hope that with simple, direct tools the people could of themselves do the rest as they have done in Wisconsin and Oregon. But the time may be too short or I may be too sanguine.

At any rate this occurs to me: that a non-partisan organization be formed to promote Popular Government, that it carry forward the propaganda till next spring and get what we can from the state legislatures and that if advisable we organize a Progressive Republican movement to finish off the job.

Personally I have little faith in the democratic party. And I have no attachment to it. I believe the insurgent movement among the republicans is bound to capture that party and that when it comes it will leave the new organization so free of interests and influences that it can go on rapidly with its work.

Here are the reasons why I feel that The Popular Government movement should be non-partisan.

1. I think the response from the people will be more immediate and more generous. I find but little to justify the belief that the people care enough for any party to resent the organization of men into a group to

promote legislation, especially when that legislation is for the sole purpose of increasing their power. Rather the people are inclined to be suspicious of any partisan organization. It suggests exclusiveness, possibly some sinister purpose and at least the chaining of big men to little or corrupt men. There is a loss of moral force in party action. We are living in a new age, which none of us understand. To day is as different from a year ago as a wheat field in June is different from a wheat field in May. The newspaper men who gather in your office offer a better guide as a referendum of popular sentiment than the men in Congress.

A non-partisan movement would get greater news support than a partisan one. It would be a call to patriotism rather than to partisanship.

Frederick C. Howe to Robert M. La Follette, 14 December 1910, La Follette Family Papers, Manuscript Division, Library of Congress, Box B64.

DOCUMENT 17   A WORKING WOMAN SEEKS THE VOTE

The campaign for woman suffrage was often seen as an effort by middle- and upper-class women only. To counteract that public impression, the advocates of suffrage sought to show lawmakers that working-class women also valued the ballot. One of these, Caroline A. Lowe of Kansas City, testified before a congressional hearing on 12 April 1912.

From the standpoint of wages received we wage earners know it to be almost universal that the men in the industries receive twice the wage granted to us, although we may be doing the same work and should have the same pay. We women work side by side with our brothers. We are children of the same parents, reared in the same homes, educated in the same schools, ride to and fro on the same early morning and late evening cars, work together the same number of hours in the same shops, and we have equal need of food, clothing and shelter. But at 21 years of age our brothers are given a powerful weapon for self-defense, a larger means for growth and self-expression.

We working women, even because we are women and find our sex not a source of strength, but a source of weakness, and offering a greater opportunity for exploitation, are denied this weapon.

Gentlemen of the committee, is there any justice underlying such a condition? If our brother workingmen are granted the ballot with which to protect themselves, do you not think that the working women should be granted this same right?

Anne F. Scott and Andrew M. Scott, eds, *One Half the People: The Fight for Woman Suffrage* (Philadelphia, Pennsylvania: J.B. Lippincott Company, 1975), pp. 123–4.

DOCUMENT 18   A BRIEF FOR HUMANITY

When Theodore Roosevelt led the Progressive party in 1912, his supporters stated the goals of reform that this third party had in mind. The following excerpt from an article written by a New York party member, William A. Prendergast, captures the spirit of their electoral appeal.

We have reached the point in our history when we realize that the nation has tremendous social, economic, and industrial problems. The solution of these problems cannot be left to the parties that shrink from accepting full responsibility for the task. If their platforms mean anything this is exactly the position of the Republican and Democratic parties. On the other hand, the Progressive platform is a frank statement of our national needs. It is a brief for humanity. It says that the interests of the individual should be the chief concern of the state. It maintains that the hours of labor, the nature of labor, the vicissitudes of labor, the responsibilities of labor and the risks to health incident to labor, are all proper subjects of governmental interest. It says that child labor must be abolished throughout the nation. It declares that women who must perform physical labor shall not work beyond their strength, and that the hours of such labor shall be limited by law, not for their sake alone, but for the future of America. It regards the natural resources of the country as a national possession and declares that they must be conserved for the benefit of all the people, and protected against private exploitation.

These are among the specific doctrines of the Progressive Party which it stands ready to incorporate into governmental law and procedure. It does not assert that it has discovered a panacea for all the ills of the body politics, but it recognizes the fact that such ills exist and it pledges itself to a determined and continued effort to cure them.

William Prendergast in the *Christian Advocate*, October 1912, quoted in Carl Resek, ed., *The Progressives* (Indianapolis, Indiana, and New York, New York: Bobbs-Merrill Company, 1967), p. 308.

DOCUMENT 19   WILLIAM ALLEN WHITE ON THE SPIRIT OF REFORM

William Allen White, editor of the Emporia Gazette *in Kansas, was one of the most famous of the midwestern progressives. In his autobiography, published in 1946, he looked back on the heyday of reform. When he mentions 'anti-pass' legislation, he is referring to attempts to regulate the practice that the railroads pursued of giving free passes or tickets to those politicians and economic leaders they wished to influence.*

But that decade which climaxed in 1912 was a time of tremendous change in our national life, particularly as it affected our national attitudes. The American people were melting down old heroes and recasting the mold in which heroes were made. Newspapers, magazines, books – every representative outlet for public opinion in the United States was turned definitely away from the scoundrels who had in the last third or quarter of the old century cast themselves in monumental brass as heroes. The muckrakers were melting it down. The people were questioning the way every rich man got his money. They were ready to believe – and too often they were justified in the belief – that he was a scamp who had pinched pennies out of the teacups of the poor by various shenanigans, who was distributing his largesse to divert attention from his rascality.

Reform was in the air. In forging new weapons of democracy in the state legislatures and in the Congress, the people were setting out on a crusade. And I was wearing the crusader's armor. A sudden new interest in the under dog was manifest in the land. He was not exalted, but universally the people began to understand what the slums were, what sweatshops were, what exploited labor was, what absentee landlordism had become in our urban life, what railroad rates were doing to the farmer and to the consumer. Two-cent railroad fares were demanded in the states. Anti-pass laws were being adopted state by state. Railroad regulation was everywhere an issue – on the stump in the legislature, in Congress. The protective tariff, as a principle, began to irk the Republican leaders of reform, chiefly because it was regarded as the bulwark of 'economic privilege' – and those two words were beginning to be common. Roosevelt was coining bitter phrases. La Follette and Bryan in the white heat of their indignation were melting rhetorical maledictions to hurl at the beneficiaries of privilege.

William Allen White, *The Autobiography of William Allen White* (New York, New York: Macmillan Company, 1946), p. 428.

DOCUMENT 20   **WOODROW WILSON ON THE PROGRESSIVE SPIRIT**

At his inauguration on 4 March 1913, Woodrow Wilson expressed the goals and social problems of the Progressive Era in lofty language that captured the spirit of moral purpose behind reform. Wilson begins by summing up the condition of the United States as he assumes the presidency.

We see that in many things that life is very great. It is incomparably great in its material aspects, in its body of wealth, in the diversity and sweep of its energy, in the industries which have been conceived and built up by the genius of individual men and the limitless enterprise of groups of men.

It is great also, very great, in its moral force. Nowhere else in the world have noble men and women exhibited in more striking forms the beauty and the energy of sympathy and helpfulness and counsel in their efforts to rectify wrong, alleviate suffering, and set the weak in the way of strength and hope. We have built up, moreover, a great system of government which has stood through a long age as in many respects a model for those who seek to set liberty upon foundations that will endure against fortuitous change, against storm and accident. Our life contains every great thing, and contains it in rich abundance.

But the evil has come with the good, and much fine gold has been corroded. With riches has come inexcusable waste. We have squandered a great part of what we might have used, and have not stopped to conserve the exceeding bounty of nature, without which our genius for enterprise would have been worthless and impotent, scorning to be careful, shamefully prodigal as well as admirably efficient. We have been proud of our industrial achievements, but we have not hitherto stopped thoughtfully enough to count the human cost, the cost of lives snuffed out, of energies overtaxed and broken, the fearful physical and spiritual cost to the men and women and children upon whom the dead weight and burden of it has fallen pitilessly the years through. The groans and agony of it all had not reached our ears, the solemn, moving undertone of our life, coming up out of the mines and factories, and out of every home where the struggle had its intimate and most familiar seat. With the great Government went many deep secret things which we too long delayed to look into and scrutinize with candid, fearless eyes. The great Government we loved has too often been made use of for private and selfish purposes, and those who had used it had forgotten the people.

Arthur S. Link, ed., *The Papers of Woodrow Wilson. Vol. 27: 1913* (Princeton, New Jersey: Princeton University Press, 1978), p. 149.

CHRONOLOGY

1890	Republicans suffer defeats in congressional elections; People's party makes gains in South and West.
1891	Populist party organizes for 1892 elections.
1892	Grover Cleveland defeats Benjamin Harrison in presidential election; Populist party makes good showing.
1893	Panic of 1893 begins in April. Cleveland summons special session in August to repeal Sherman Silver Purchase Act.
1894	Pullman Strike and Coxey's Army express unrest with the economic hard times. Republicans make big gains in congressional elections.
1895	Hard times continue. Anti-Saloon League founded.
1896	Case of *Plessy* v. *Ferguson* upholds segregation. Bryan delivers Cross of Gold Speech and wins Democratic nomination. William McKinley (Republican) is elected president.
1897	Prosperity returns. Dingley Tariff enacted.
1898	Spanish–American War sees United States emerge victorious and acquire overseas empire. Theodore Roosevelt elected governor of New York State.
1899	Acquisition of the Philippine Islands. Fears of trusts grow.
1900	McKinley defeats Bryan in second race for the White House. Robert M. La Follette elected governor of Wisconsin. Galveston hurricane death toll sparks interest in municipal reform.
1901	William McKinley assassinated. Theodore Roosevelt becomes president.
1902	Roosevelt has Justice Department file Northern Securities case. President settles anthracite coal strike. Muckraking journalism is launched.
1903	United States acquires Panama Canal Zone.
1904	Theodore Roosevelt elected president in his own right; says that he will not seek another term in 1908.

1905	Investigations of insurance frauds in New York State and influence of public utilities spark popular outrage.
	Roosevelt launches campaign for railroad regulation.
1906	Congress passes Hepburn Act to regulate the railroads as well as Meat Inspection law and Pure Food and Drug Act.
	Roosevelt attacks muckraking journalists.
1907	Panic of 1907 stimulates interest in banking reform.
1908	Taft defeats Bryan in the presidential election.
1909	Roosevelt leaves for African safari.
	Taft deals with Payne–Aldrich Tariff.
	Ballinger–Pinchot controversy begins.
1910	Roosevelt returns from Europe and announces New Nationalism at Osawatomie, Kansas.
	Republicans lose control of the House of Representatives to the Democrats.
	Woodrow Wilson elected governor of New Jersey.
1911	Triangle Fire in New York indicates need for social justice.
	Taft–Roosevelt split widens.
1912	Roosevelt challenges Taft for Republican nomination and loses; decides to run as Progressive party candidate.
	Democrats nominate Woodrow Wilson for president.
	Four-cornered race ensues among Roosevelt, Wilson, Taft and Eugene V. Debs.
	New Nationalism and New Freedom are opposing philosophies in election.
	Wilson elected president.
1913	Suffrage parade precedes Wilson inauguration.
	Webb–Kenyon Act passed to regulate shipments of liquor in interstate commerce.
	Underwood Tariff enacted with income tax.
	Federal Reserve Law passed.
1914	Clayton Antitrust Act passed.
	Federal Trade Commission Act passed.
	World War I breaks out in Europe.

GLOSSARY

Anti-Saloon League   A pressure group formed in 1895 to pursue the restriction of alcohol by means of limiting and eventually eliminating the saloon and liquor dealers from business.

antitrust   The doctrine that monopolies presented a danger to the American economy and should be broken up through lawsuits sponsored by the government.

Ballinger–Pinchot controversy   Dispute of 1909–10 between Secretary of the Interior Richard A. Ballinger and Chief Forester Gifford Pinchot over the direction of conservation policy.

city manager form of city government   Derived from the commission form of city government (see below), this approach to urban reform vested power in a nonpartisan executive who ran the city like a business.

Clayton Antitrust Act (1914)   Enacted during the Wilson administration to strengthen enforcement of the original antitrust law of 1890.

Commission form of city government   A reform device that took power away from geographically based units in the city or town and shifted authority to commissioners representing the whole municipality.

Democratic party   The oldest American party, it stood for limited government and state rights in 1890 and was strongest in the South between 1890 and 1914.

Dingley Tariff Law (1897)   A high-tariff law enacted during the McKinley administration that became associated with prosperity in the minds of conservatives and with the need for tariff reform among progressives.

direct primary   Instead of having candidates chosen at party conventions where 'bosses' exercised a major influence, members of the party would participate in elections that would select the nominees for state and national office.

Federal Reserve Act   Passed in 1913, it established a Federal Reserve Board that acted as a kind of central bank for the United States through twelve regional banks across the country.

free silver   A shortened form of the phrase 'the free and unlimited coinage of silver into money at a ratio of 16 to 1 with gold.' Such a monetary policy would have produced inflation that would have benefited the debt-ridden South and West.

Hepburn Act (1906)   Endorsed by Theodore Roosevelt, it broadened the power of the Interstate Commerce Commission over railroad rates.

immigration restriction   Proponents argued that the United States was allowing too many immigrants who were not qualified to become citizens into the country. This position was usually justified on grounds of racial, religious, or ethnocultural prejudice.

initiative   A procedure that would allow voters to ask the legislature to enact a specific law if enough signatures were obtained. It was designed to offset the power of lobbies in the state legislatures.

Interstate Commerce Commission (1887)   A regulatory agency charged with the task of overseeing the nation's railroads.

muckraking   A term devised by Theodore Roosevelt to describe journalists who investigated issues of corruption and scandal. It has become a generic term for such reporting.

National American Woman Suffrage Association   The main lobbying organization for woman suffrage between 1890 and 1914.

Northern Securities Case (1902–4)   The prosecution by the Justice Department of a combination of railroads in the Northwest. This became the way that Theodore Roosevelt established his reputation as a trust-buster.

Panic of 1893   The economic crisis that led to a prolonged depression during the mid-1890s.

Panic of 1907   A shorter economic downturn that focused attention on the state of the American banking system.

Payne–Aldrich Tariff (1909)   A tariff measure that failed to meet popular expectations for lower rates and produced political discord for the Taft administration that had favored the law.

People's party (or Populists)   Agrarian-based protest party that flourished in the South and West between 1890 and 1897. It was associated with the doctrine of free silver.

Plessy v. Ferguson (1896)   The Supreme Court case that upheld racial segregation laws in the American South.

Progressive party (1912–16)   The third party that Theodore Roosevelt formed in 1912 when he ran for president.

progressives   A general term for those who favored some degree of reform in the United States between 1895 and 1915.

prohibition   A campaign popular in the South and West to bar the sale or manufacture of alcoholic beverages throughout the United States.

Pure Food and Drug Act (1906)   A measure to regulate the medicines that consumers bought over-the-counter and the meats and other processed foods that they used.

recall   A method whereby voters could decide to call an election to remove an official for unpopular or unwise decisions. It also included provision to overturn a judicial decision through an election.

referendum   Allowing the voters of a city or state to vote to decide the merits of a disputed issue rather than relying on a legislature to decide the question.

regulatory agency   A panel of experts, usually appointed, who comprised an agency designed to supervise an industry or social problem. The Interstate Commerce Commission offered a good example of such an agency.

Republican party   Party which advocated the use of government to promote economic growth through protective tariffs and assistance to business in the 1890s. It became hostile to regulation after 1900 despite the efforts of Theodore Roosevelt and a progressive wing.

segregation   The doctrine of legalized racial separation that became standard in the treatment of African Americans throughout the American South in the 1890s. Endorsed by the Supreme Court ruling in the *Plessy* v. *Ferguson* case of 1896.

settlement houses   Institutions located in American cities where social workers lived in the neighborhoods and sought to help residents improve their lives. Associated with Jane Addams in Chicago at Hull House, though many others participated in other cities.

Sherman Antitrust Act (1890)   Passed to curb the growth of corporate monopoly, it was an important regulatory law in the Progressive Era.

Social Gospel   The doctrine that religious denominations had an obligation to pursue a more just and equitable society by dealing with important issues, ministering to the poor, and assisting government in improving the quality of life.

standpatter   Based on the poker phrase when a player 'stands pat' with a good hand, it referred to conservatives, usually Republicans, who opposed change because times were good and regulatory laws were unneeded.

Underwood Tariff (1913)   A Democratic tariff reform bill of the Wilson administration. It was most notable for imposing the first modern income tax.

Webb–Kenyon Act (1913)   Prohibited the shipping of liquor from a state where drinking was allowed into a state that had banned the sale of alcoholic beverages.

woman suffrage   The campaign to extend the vote to women that was pursued between 1890 and 1914.

WHO'S WHO

Addams, Jane (1860–1935) Founder of Hull House and one of the most famous women reformers of the Progressive Era.

Aldrich, Nelson W. (1841–1915) Republican senator from Rhode Island and leader of the conservatives in the Senate.

Baker, Ray Stannard (1870–1946) Muckraker and friend of Roosevelt and Wilson.

Brandeis, Louis Dembitz (1856–1941) Known as 'The People's Lawyer' and the architect of Woodrow Wilson's 'New Freedom' in 1912.

Bryan, William Jennings (1860–1925) Three-time presidential candidate of the Democratic party (1896, 1900, 1908) and Secretary of State under Woodrow Wilson.

Cannon, Joseph Gurney (1836–1926) Republican Speaker of the House of Representatives 1903–11, and leading opponent of Theodore Roosevelt's reforms.

Catt, Carrie Chapman (1859–1947) President of the National American Woman Suffrage Association 1900–4 and major figure in the suffrage struggle.

Debs, Eugene Victor (1855–1926) Presidential candidate of the Socialist party, 1900–12.

Du Bois, William Edward Burghardt (1868–1963) Founder of the National Association for the Advancement of Colored People and leading black intellectual of the early twentieth century.

Hanna, Marcus Alonzo (1837–1904) Cleveland industrialist who was McKinley's campaign manager in 1896 and later senator from Ohio.

Hughes, Charles Evans (1862–1948) Lawyer who became Governor of New York in the 1906 election and was rival to Taft for the nomination in 1908; later Supreme Court Justice and Republican presidential candidate in 1916.

Jones, Samuel M. 'Golden Rule' (1846–1904) Reform mayor of Toledo, Ohio, identified with Christian socialism.

La Follette, Robert Marion (1855–1925) Governor and senator from Wisconsin; a leading progressive reformer.

McClure, Samuel Sidney (1857–1949) Owner of *McClure's Magazine* who sponsored muckraking journalism.

McKinley, William (1843–1901)   Twenty-fifth President of the United States from 1897 to 1901.

Paul, Alice (1885–1977)   Founder of the Congressional Union, a militant arm of the woman suffrage movement that became the National Woman's Party.

Pingree, Hazen (1840–1901)   Reform mayor of Detroit, Michigan and later governor of the state.

Roosevelt, Theodore (1858–1919)   Twenty-sixth President of the United States from 1901 to 1909 and Progressive party presidential candidate in 1912 associated with the New Nationalism.

Steffens, Lincoln (1866–1936)   A leading muckraking journalist whose major work was *The Shame of the Cities* (1904).

Taft, William Howard (1857–1930)   Twenty-seventh President of the United States, who split with Theodore Roosevelt and lost his race for re-election in 1912 against Roosevelt and Woodrow Wilson.

Tarbell, Ida (1857–1944)   A preeminent muckraker whose history of Standard Oil became an influential example of the genre.

Washington, Booker T. (1856–1915)   The most famous and important African American leader of the Progressive Era.

White, William Allen (1868–1944)   Editor of the *Emporia (Kansas) Gazette*, sometime muckraker and progressive ally of Theodore Roosevelt.

Wilson, Woodrow (1856–1924)   Twenty-eighth President of the United States, who was identified with the program called the New Freedom.

BIBLIOGRAPHY

Any brief bibliography of the United States in the Progressive Era must be selective. The titles that follow will help guide the interested student into the rich sources in this period of United States history. The brief comments about the titles are designed to provide guidance about which sources will be most helpful.

COLLECTIONS OF PRINTED DOCUMENTS

1   Walter Johnson, ed., *Selected Letters of William Allen White, 1899–1943*, New York, New York: Henry Holt and Company, 1947. The letters of one of the most prominent midwestern progressives.

2   Arthur S. Link *et al.*, eds, *The Papers of Woodrow Wilson*, 69 vols, Princeton, New Jersey: Princeton University Press, 1966–93. A superb collection which provides insights into every aspect of American reform.

3   Elting E. Morison *et al.*, eds, *The Letters of Theodore Roosevelt*, 8 vols, Cambridge, Massachusetts: Harvard University Press, 1951–54. The letters that Theodore Roosevelt sent out which are significant for his opinions on the major issues of the period.

4   Carl Resek, ed., *The Progressives*, Indianapolis, Indiana: Bobbs Merrill, 1967. A useful collection of primary documents.

5   Ella Winter and Granville Hicks, eds, *The Letters of Lincoln Steffens,* New York, New York: Harcourt Brace, 1938. The letters of the leading practitioner of muckraking journalism.

AUTOBIOGRAPHIES, MEMOIRS, AND DIARIES

6   Jane Addams, *Twenty Years at Hull House*, New York, New York: Macmillan Company, 1910. The memoirs of the woman who pioneered in the settlement house movement.

7   Ray Stannard Baker, *American Chronicle*, New York, New York: Charles Scribner's Sons, 1946. Baker was a muckraker and biographer of Woodrow Wilson, and his memoirs are a fascinating account of his career.

8   Richard T. Ely, *Ground Under Our Feet*, New York, New York: Macmillan, 1938. Ely was one of the academics who called for a greater governmental role.

9   Robert M. La Follette, *La Follette's Autobiography*, Madison, Wisconsin: The Robert M. La Follette Company, 1913. La Follette's autobiography is also an extended attack on Theodore Roosevelt's claim to be a progressive leader. This is an important document for understanding progressivism.

10 Gifford Pinchot, *Breaking New Ground*, Seattle, Washington: University of Washington Press, 1972. Pinchot was a significant leader in the conservation cause, and his autobiography reveals his close ties with Roosevelt. The book also underscores the differences between Progressive Era conservation and modern environmentalism.

11 Theodore Roosevelt, *The Autobiography of Theodore Roosevelt*, New York, New York: Outlook Printing Company, 1913. In this autobiography, Roosevelt is determined to show that William Howard Taft had betrayed the Roosevelt legacy as president. The book is also crucial for understanding Roosevelt's approach to the presidential office.

12 Lincoln Steffens, *The Autobiography of Lincoln Steffens*, New York, New York: Harcourt Brace, 1931. This is one of the great memoirs of the period with a riveting account of Steffens's journey from progressivism to pro-communist sympathies in the 1920s. The book is infused with the moralism and sense of outrage at a sinful world that animated so much of American reform.

13 Ida Tarbell, *All in a Day's Work*, New York, New York: Macmillan Company, 1939. Tarbell moved from muckraking to pro-business journalism, and this book describes that transition.

14 William Allen White, *The Autobiography of William Allen White*, New York, New York: The Macmillan Company, 1946. White was a very popular editor, a sometime muckraker, and close ally of Theodore Roosevelt. The spirit of the reform era comes through very well in his emotional remembrance of his youthful foray into reform politics.

GENERAL BOOKS

15 Daniel Aaron, *Men of Good Hope,* New York, New York: Oxford University Press, 1951. An influential survey of progressive thinking written just after World War II.

16 Edward L. Ayers, *The Promise of the New South: Life After Reconstruction*, New York, New York: Oxford University Press, 1992. An excellent and comprehensive treatment of the development of the South after 1877. Very useful for its notes and analytic insights.

17 John D. Buenker, *Urban Liberalism and Progressive Reform*, New York, New York: Charles Scribner's Sons, 1973. Argues that reform was urban-based and illustrates that thesis by examining the passage of social justice and regulatory legislation in the industrial states of the Northeast and Middle West.

18 John D. Buenker, John C. Burnham, and Robert M. Crunden, *Progressivism*, Cambridge, Massachusetts: Schenkman Publishing Company, 1977. Three historians offer contrasting interpretations of what progressivism was and what its impact was on American history.

19 John D. Buenker and Edward R. Kantowicz, eds, *Historical Dictionary of the Progressive Era, 1890–1920*, Westport, Connecticut: Greenwood Press, 1988. A useful and well-done compendium of information on a variety of topics, individuals, and laws relating to the reform era.

20 Charles W. Calhoun, ed., *The Gilded Age: Essays on the Origins of Modern America,* Wilmington, Delaware: Scholarly Resources, 1996. An excellent collection of essays by experts on the late nineteenth century into various important aspects of the nation's history.

21 Robert W. Cherny, *American Politics in the Gilded Age, 1868–1900,* Wheeling, Illinois: Harlan Davidson, 1997. An up-to-date survey of the issues and literature dealing with politics at the end of the nineteenth century. The bibliography is very helpful for further research.

22 Gene Clanton, *Populism: The Humane Preference in America, 1890–1900,* Boston, Massachusetts: Twayne Publishers, 1991. A sympathetic and well-informed treatment of the agrarian protest movement that so disrupted and reshaped American politics in the 1890s.

23 Gene Clanton, *Congressional Populism and the Crisis of the 1890s,* Lawrence, Kansas: University Press of Kansas, 1998. A close look at the performance of the relatively small group of Populist lawmakers who actually sat in the House of Representatives and the Senate.

24 John Milton Cooper, Jr., *Pivotal Decades: The United States, 1900–1920,* New York, New York: W.W. Norton, 1990. A very comprehensive and readable survey of the period by one of the best historians of this phase of American history. Cooper is especially good on Woodrow Wilson and his reform credentials.

25 Robert M. Crunden, *Ministers of Reform: The Progressives' Achievement in American Civilization,* New York, New York: Basic Books, 1982. An influential study of the role of religious upbringing and evangelical motives in the lives of some key progressives.

26 Steven J. Diner, *A Very Different Age: Americans of the Progressive Era,* New York, New York: Hill and Wang, 1998. Reflecting the newer historical scholarship, Diner's book devotes more time to the actual experience of Americans during the Progressive Era than he does to political events. Very helpful for the social history of the early twentieth century.

27 Melvyn Dubofsky, *Industrialism and the American Worker, 1865–1920, 2nd edn,* Arlington Heights, Illinois: Harlan Davidson, 1985. An interpretive survey of the place of labor in the Progressive Era.

28 Lewis L. Gould, *Reform and Regulation: American Politics From Roosevelt to Wilson,* Prospect Heights, Illinois: Waveland Press, 1996. A narrative about the political events of the early twentieth century.

29 Lewis L. Gould, ed., *The Progressive Era,* Syracuse, New York: Syracuse University Press, 1974. A collection of essays about various phases of reform and its impact on the United States. The essay on the legacy of progressivism by Thomas K. McCraw is particularly useful.

30 Dewey Grantham, *Southern Progressivism: The Reconciliation of Progress and Tradition,* Knoxville, Tennessee: University of Tennessee Press, 1983. A very thorough and comprehensive examination of the impact of reform on the South.

31 Richard Hofstadter, *The Age of Reform,* New York, New York: Alfred A. Knopf, 1956. One of the most important books ever written on the history of American reform. Even though it is now dated in its use of sources, Hofstadter's work contains many insights and repays careful reading.

32 Gabriel Kolko, *The Triumph of Conservatism: A Reinterpretation of American History, 1900–1916*, New York, New York: Macmillan, 1963. An interpretation from the left that had a great deal of impact on scholarship about this period in the 1960s.

33 J. Morgan Kousser, *The Shaping of Southern Politics: Suffrage Restriction and the Establishment of the One-Party South, 1880–1910*, New Haven, Connecticut: Yale University Press, 1974. A state-by-state examination of how southern whites used the electoral machinery to remove blacks from politics during this period.

34 Arthur S. Link, *Woodrow Wilson and the Progressive Era*, New York, New York: Harper & Row, 1956. Link was the preeminent biographer of Woodrow Wilson who became more favorable to his subject as time passed. This book is a very helpful summary of his findings at a time before his respect for Wilson reached adulatory levels.

35 Arthur S. Link and Richard McCormick, *Progressivism*, Arlington Heights, Illinois: Harlan Davidson, 1983. Link teamed with a then younger scholar to produce a very crisp and analytic treatment of the course of the progressive spirit.

36 Michael McGerr, *The Decline of Popular Politics: The American North, 1865–1928*, New York, New York: Oxford University Press, 1986. An important examination of the ways in which Americans conducted their political campaigns and how that process changed from the Gilded Age to the Progressive Era.

37 Henry F. May, *The End of American Innocence*, New York, New York: Alfred A. Knopf, 1959. May argues that the changes usually associated with the 1920s in American culture actually showed themselves before the onset of World War I.

38 Gwendolyn Mink, *Old Labor and New Immigrants in American Political Development: Union, Party, and State, 1875–1920*, Ithaca, New York: Cornell University Press, 1986. A thorough treatment of the role of organized labor during the political battles of the period.

39 H. Wayne Morgan, *From Hayes to McKinley: National Party Politics, 1877–1896*, Syracuse, New York: Syracuse University Press, 1969. An excellent and well-written treatment of the political history of the late nineteenth century.

40 George E. Mowry, *The Era of Theodore Roosevelt*, New York, New York: Harper & Row, 1958. Mowry was a pioneer in the study of Theodore Roosevelt as a national politician, and this book is an outstanding summary of his impact on the Republican party.

41 Nell Irvin Painter, *Standing at Armageddon: The United States, 1877–1919*, New York, New York: W.W. Norton, 1987. An overview of the era from a point of view that is critical of the performance of American society.

42 Daniel T. Rodgers, *Atlantic Crossings: Social Politics in a Progressive Age*, Cambridge, Massachusetts: Belknap Press of Harvard University Press, 1998. Emphasizes the interplay between Europe and the United States in the development of reform programs.

43 David Sarasohn, *The Party of Reform: Democrats in the Progressive Era*, Jackson, Mississippi: University of Mississippi Press, 1989. Argues forcefully that the Democrats did more to advance reform than did the Republicans. A well-researched and interesting interpretation.

44   Stephen Skowronek, *Building a New American State: The Expansion of National Administrative Capacities, 1877–1920,* New York, New York: Cambridge University Press, 1982. Looks at various aspects of the government to show how the power of the national state grew.

45   Mark Summers, *The Gilded Age: or The Hazard of New Functions,* Upper Saddle River, New Jersey: Prentice Hall, 1997. A lively examination of the late nineteenth century.

46   Richard L. Watson, Jr., *The Development of National Power: The United States, 1900–1919,* Boston, Massachusetts: Houghton Mifflin, 1976. An older book but one that is packed with useful information about important subjects relating to the expansion of the federal government.

47   Robert Wiebe, *Businessmen and Reform: A Study of the Progressive Movement* Cambridge, Massachusetts: Harvard University Press, 1962. An important early account of the role of business in driving reform ideas.

48   Robert Wiebe, *The Search for Order, 1877–1920,* New York, New York: Hill and Wang, 1967. A very influential analysis of the Gilded Age and Progressive Era that has many provocative ideas.

49   R. Hal Williams, *Years of Decision: American Politics in the 1890s,* Prospect Heights, Illinois: Waveland Press, 1993. The best survey of American politics during the 1890s written in a lively and engaging manner.

50   C. Vann Woodward, *Origins of the New South, 1877–1913,* Baton Rouge, Louisiana: Louisiana State University Press, 1951. A masterful treatment of the South, and one of the most important and influential books on American history in the second half of the twentieth century.

STATE STUDIES

51   Richard M. Abrams, *Conservatism in a Progressive Era: Massachusetts Politics, 1900–1912,* Cambridge, Massachusetts: Harvard University Press, 1964. Looks at a key state in the Northeast and explains why Massachusetts was not as sympathetic to reform as its midwestern counterparts.

52   Robert W. Cherny, *Populism, Progressivism, and the Transformation of Nebraska Politics, 1885–1915,* Lincoln, Nebraska: University of Nebraska Press, 1981. Uses voting behavior analysis and other sources to consider the state where William Jennings Bryan had his base and the Populists were also strong.

53   Lewis L. Gould, *Progressives and Prohibitionists: Texas Democrats in the Wilson Era,* Austin, Texas: Texas State Historical Association, 1992. Argues that the crusade against liquor represented a progressive reform in this southwestern state.

54   Sheldon Hackney, *Populism to Progressivism in Alabama,* Princeton, New Jersey: Princeton University Press, 1969. Considers the shift from agrarian reform in the 1890s to the Democratic campaigns for change after 1900.

55   Robert Sherman LaForte, *Leaders of Reform: Progressive Republicans in Kansas, 1900–1916,* Lawrence, Kansas: University Press of Kansas, 1974. A thorough review of a significant state in the Midwest where reform was pervasive.

56   William A. Link, *The Paradox of Southern Progressivism, 1880–1930*, Chapel Hill, North Carolina: University of North Carolina Press, 1992. A survey of the course of reform in the South.

57   Richard L. McCormick, *From Realignment to Reform: Political Change in New York State, 1893–1910*, Ithaca, New York: Cornell University Press, 1981. A judicious and perceptive treatment of the battles between reformers and conservatives in the nation's most populous state.

58   Herbert F. Margulies, *The Decline of the Progressive Movement in Wisconsin, 1890–1920*, Madison, Wisconsin: State Historical Society of Wisconsin, 1968. Rare in covering the whole process from the rise of the progressive spirit to the reasons for its decline by the onset of World War I.

59   David P. Thelen, *The New Citizenship: Origins of Progressivism in Wisconsin, 1885–1900*, Columbia, Missouri: University of Missouri Press, 1972. An important interpretation of the origins of reform and its relationship to the career of Robert M. La Follette.

BIOGRAPHIES

60   John M. Blum, *The Republican Roosevelt*, Cambridge, Massachusetts: Harvard University Press, 1954. A brilliant brief treatment of Roosevelt's career. This book influenced a generation and more of writing about this significant president.

61   Kendrick Clements, *The Presidency of Woodrow Wilson*, Lawrence, Kansas: University Press of Kansas, 1992. A very well done examination of Wilson's administration and his impact on the presidency.

62   John Milton Cooper, *The Warrior and the Priest: Woodrow Wilson and Theodore Roosevelt*, Cambridge, Massachusetts: Harvard University Press, 1983. An interesting comparative study of the two progressive presidents. Cooper is more favorable to Wilson than to Roosevelt.

63   Allen F. Davis, *American Heroine: The Life and Legend of Jane Addams*, New York, New York: Oxford University Press, 1973. A very thorough biography of Addams that shows her important role in reform.

64   Lewis L. Gould, *The Presidency of William McKinley*, Lawrence, Kansas: University Press of Kansas, 1980. Argues that McKinley created the modern presidency during and after the war with Spain in 1898.

65   Lewis L. Gould, *The Presidency of Theodore Roosevelt*, Lawrence, Kansas: University Press of Kansas, 1991. Considers the ways in which Roosevelt strengthened and personalized the presidency for Americans during the first decade of the twentieth century.

66   Louis R. Harlan, *Booker T. Washington: The Wizard of Tuskegee*, New York, New York: Oxford University Press, 1983. A superb study of the most important African American. Harlan does justice to the complexity of Washington's character and the problems he faced within a segregated society.

67   Louis Koenig, *Bryan: A Political Biography of William Jennings Bryan*, New York, New York: G.P. Putnam's Sons, 1971. The best biography of Bryan that puts him in his political context.

68   Arthur S. Link, *Wilson*, 5 vols, Princeton, New Jersey: Princeton University Press, 1947–65. Link began a multi-volume biography of Wilson that he never finished because of his involvement with editing Wilson's papers. The first volume is critical of Wilson, and the succeeding ones are more favorable. Nonetheless, every student of Wilson owes an immense debt to Link's pioneering scholarship.

69   Herbert F. Margulies, *Reconciliation and Revival: James R. Mann and the House Republicans in the Wilson Era*, Westport, Connecticut: Greenwood Press, 1996. One of the few biographies of a Republican House member, this book contains an abundance of information about the inner workings of legislative politics.

70   Nick Salvatore, *Eugene V. Debs: Citizen and Socialist,* Urbana, Illinois: University of Illinois Press, 1982. The best one-volume biography of the Socialist leader.

71   Kathryn Kish Sklar, *Florence Kelley and the Nation's Work. Vol. 1: The Rise of Women's Political Culture, 1830–1900,* New Haven, Connecticut: Yale University Press, 1995. The first of two volumes on this important social reformer and advocate of better working conditions for laboring people.

72   Jean Strouse, *Morgan: American Financier*, New York, New York: Random House, 1999. A new biography of J.P. Morgan based on his papers. Strouse is an admirer of Morgan and the book does not adequately assess the criticisms of Morgan's dominance within the American economy.

73   David P. Thelen, *Robert M. La Follette and the Insurgent Spirit,* Boston, Massachusetts: Little, Brown and Company, 1976. A good brief study, but La Follette still needs a major biographical treatment.

74   Richard E. Welch, Jr., *The Presidencies of Grover Cleveland*, Lawrence, Kansas: University Press of Kansas, 1988. Excellent on Cleveland and his political problems in the White House.

AFRICAN AMERICANS

75   Leon F. Litwack, *Trouble In Mind: Black Southerners in the Age of Jim Crow*, New York, New York: Alfred A. Knopf, 1998. An excellent and harrowing account of the situation of African Americans in the South in the decades following Reconstruction.

76   John D. Weaver, *The Brownsville Raid*, College Station, Texas: Texas A&M University Press, 1992 (reprint of original 1970 edition). Details the miscarriage of justice that African-American soldiers experienced when Theodore Roosevelt discharged them from the service for their alleged participation in a shooting incident in Brownsville, Texas, in 1906. A graphic study of a segregated society at work.

77   Joel Williamson, *The Crucible of Race: Black–White Relations in the American South Since Emancipation*, New York, New York: Oxford University Press, 1984. An incisive study of the varieties of racism that animated the South in the years after 1877.

78   C. Vann Woodward, *The Strange Career of Jim Crow*, New York, New York: Oxford University Press, 1955. A masterful account of the rise of segregation, and a book that has stimulated a scholarly controversy about its thesis during the last half century.

REGULATORY ISSUES

79 Samuel P. Hays, *Conservation and the Gospel of Efficiency: The Progressive Conservation Movement, 1890–1920*, Cambridge, Massachusetts: Harvard University Press, 1959. A detailed examination of the development of conservation as an issue during the Progressive Era.

80 Gabriel Kolko, *Railroads and Regulation, 1877–1916*, Princeton, New Jersey: Princeton University Press, 1965. Contends that the railroads actually welcomed regulation as a way of eliminating threats from the states. The thesis is not in the end convincing.

81 Thomas K. McCraw, *Prophets of Regulation: Charles Francis Adams, Louis D. Brandeis, James M. Landis, Alfred E. Kahn*, Cambridge, Massachusetts: Harvard University Press, 1984. The chapter on Brandeis provides one of the best discussions in print of the nature of the American economy in the early twentieth century.

82 Albro Martin, *Enterprise Denied: Origins of the Decline of American Railroads, 1893–1917*, New York, New York: Columbia University Press, 1971. The mirror image of Kolko's book on railroad regulation, Martin asserts that the railroads faced too much regulation that crippled their ability to survive economically.

83 James L. Penick, Jr., *Progressive Politics and Conservation: The Ballinger–Pinchot Affair*, Chicago, Illinois: University of Chicago Press, 1968. A crisp narrative about this conservation controversy that has implications beyond its immediate topic.

84 Martin J. Sklar, *The Corporate Reconstruction of American Capitalism, 1890–1916: The Market, the Law, and Politics*, New York, New York: Cambridge University Press, 1988. Uses Roosevelt's effort to achieve antitrust legislation in 1908 as a vehicle for exploring business–government relations in the Progressive Era. Written from the left and very critical of politicians and business leaders.

85 Hans B. Thorelli, *The Federal Antitrust Policy: Origination of an American Tradition*, Baltimore, Maryland: Johns Hopkins University Press, 1955. More encyclopedic than riveting, but the book contains a wealth of information about American attitudes toward the trusts and their regulation.

URBAN REFORM

86 Melvin G. Holli, *Reform in Detroit: Hazen S. Pingree and Urban Politics*, New York, New York: Oxford University Press, 1969. An examination of the mayor of Detroit in the 1890s that is also important because of the distinction it makes between structural reformers who wanted to change the process by which the city was governed and social reformers who wanted more sweeping alterations in the substance of policy.

87 Rivka Shpak Lissak, *Pluralism and Progressives: Hull House and the New Immigrants, 1890–1919*, Chicago, Illinois: University of Chicago Press, 1989. Examines the attitudes of settlement house workers and leaders toward the new immigrants in the growing cities of the early twentieth century.

88 Raymond A. Mohl, *The New City: Urban America in the Industrial Age*, Arlington Heights, Illinois: Harlan Davidson, 1985. A good summary of the ways in which urbanization changed the face of American society.

89 Bradley Rice, *Progressive Cities: The Commission Government Movement in America, 1901–1920*, Austin, Texas: University of Texas Press, 1977. An excellent brief account of the commission government and city manager reforms.

90 Martin J. Schiesl, *The Politics of Efficiency: Municipal Administration and Reform in America, 1880–1920*, Berkeley, California: University of California Press, 1977. An influential treatment of municipal reform.

WOMAN SUFFRAGE AND WOMEN'S ISSUES

91 Rebecca Edwards, *Angels in the Machinery: Gender in American Party Politics from the Civil War to the Progressive Era*, New York, New York: Oxford University Press, 1997. A younger scholar considers the impact of women and gender issues on political events before the achievement of suffrage.

92 Ellen Fitzpatrick, *Endless Crusade: Women Social Scientists and Progressive Reform*, New York, New York: Oxford University Press, 1990. Looks at the career of three women social scientists to gauge their impact on reform issues.

93 Eleanor Flexner and Ellen Fitzpatrick, *Century of Struggle: The Woman's Rights Movement in the United States,* Cambridge, Massachusetts: Harvard University Press, revised and enlarged edition, 1996. The standard treatment of how women achieved the vote.

94 Glenda Elizabeth Gilmore, *Gender and Jim Crow: Women and Politics of White Supremacy in North Carolina, 1896–1920*, Chapel Hill, North Carolina: University of North Carolina Press, 1996. An important new study that looks at issues of race and gender as they affected women in a key southern state.

95 Sara Hunter Graham, *Woman Suffrage and the New Democracy,* New Haven, Connecticut: Yale University Press, 1996. An incisive study of the National American Woman Suffrage Association.

96 Aileen Kraditor, *The Ideas of the Woman Suffrage Movement, 1890–1920,* New York, New York: Doubleday, 1971. One of the pioneering treatments of woman suffrage that focuses on the ideology of the movement.

97 Christine Lunardini, *From Equal Suffrage to Equal Rights: Alice Paul and the National Woman's Party, 1910–1928,* New York, New York: New York University Press, 1986. A book that considers suffrage from the perspective of one of its most radical advocates, Alice Paul.

98 Theda Skocpol, *Protecting Soldiers and Mothers: The Political Origins of Social Policy in the United States*, Cambridge, Massachusetts: Harvard University Press, 1992. A very influential analysis of how the desire to protect veterans after the Civil War helped prepare the way for addressing the problems of some women.

PROHIBITION

99 Jack S. Blocker, Jr., *Retreat from Reform: The Prohibition Movement in the United States, 1890–1913*, Westport, Connecticut: Greenwood Press, 1976. A critical survey of the motives of the prohibitionists.

100 Richard F. Hamm, *Shaping the Eighteenth Amendment: Temperance Reform, Legal Culture, and the Polity, 1880–1920*, Chapel Hill, North Carolina: University of North Carolina Press, 1995. Examines the adoption of prohibition as an episode in federal–state relations.

101 K. Austin Kerr, *Organized for Prohibition: A New History of the Anti-Saloon League*, New Haven, Connecticut: Yale University Press, 1985. Excellent on the major pressure group that achieved prohibition.

102 James Timberlake, *Prohibition and the Progressive Movement*, Cambridge, Massachusetts: Harvard University Press, 1963. An older book, but still useful for making the case that prohibition was an integral part of progressive reform.

ARTICLES

103 Howard W. Allen, Aage R. Clausen, and Jerome M. Clubb, 'Political Reform and Negro Rights in the Senate, 1909–1915,' *Journal of Southern History*, 37 (1971): 191–212. Looks at the place of African-American issues in the Congress.

104 Howard W. Allen and Jerome Clubb, 'Progressive Reform and the Political System,' *Pacific Northwest Quarterly*, 65 (1974): 130–45. Contends that progressivism was not based on an upsurge of electoral support.

105 Paula Baker, 'The Domestication of Politics: Women and American Political Society, 1780–1920,' *American Historical Review*, 89 (1984): 620–47. An extended examination of how women fitted into politics at the end of the nineteenth century.

106 Peter G. Filene, 'An Obituary for the Progressive Movement,' *American Quarterly*, 22 (1970): 20–34. A famous demolition of the contributions of progressivism as an idea for historians to use.

107 Samuel P. Hays, 'The Politics of Reform in Municipal Government in the Progressive Era,' *Pacific Northwest Quarterly*, 55 (October, 1964): 157–69. One of the most influential articles about the period. It argued that municipal reform often had a class basis and a hidden agenda of social change. This essay has been reprinted many times.

108 Richard L. McCormick, 'The Discovery that Business Corrupts Politics: A Reappraisal of the Origins of Progressivism,' *American Historical Review*, 86 (1981): 242–74. Focuses on the 1905–6 period to discuss the public outrage at corruption and the resulting support for reform.

109 Eileen McDonagh, 'The "Welfare Rights State" and the "Civil Rights State": Policy Paradox and State Building in the Progressive Era,' *Studies in American Political Development*, 7 (1993): 225–74. A political scientist looks at progressivism.

110 Daniel T. Rodgers, 'In Search of Progressivism,' in Stanley I. Kutler and Stanley N. Katz, eds, *The Promise of American History: Progress and Prospects*, Baltimore, Maryland: Johns Hopkins University Press, 1982, pp. 113–32. A good review of the literature and issues surrounding progressivism.

111 Martin J. Sklar, 'Periodization and Historiography: Studying American Political Development in the Progressive Era, 1890s–1916,' *Studies in American Political Development*, 5 (1991): 173–213. Another recent historical critique of the writings about progressive reform.

112 James Weinstein, 'Organized Business and the City Commission and Manager Movements,' *Journal of Southern History*, 28 (1962): 166–82. Contends that business interests pushed for municipal reform.

INDEX

SEMINAR STUDIES IN HISTORY

General Editors: Clive Emsley & Gordon Martel

The series was founded by Patrick Richardson in 1966. Between 1980 and 1996 Roger Lockyer edited the series before handing over to Clive Emsley (Professor of History at the Open University) and Gordon Martel (Professor of International History at the University of Northern British Columbia, Canada and Senior Research Fellow at De Montfort University).

MEDIEVAL ENGLAND

The Pre-Reformation Church in England 1400–1530 (Second edition)
Christopher Harper-Bill   0 582 28989 0

Lancastrians and Yorkists: The Wars of the Roses
David R Cook   0 582 35384 X

TUDOR ENGLAND

Henry VII (Third edition)
Roger Lockyer & Andrew Thrush   0 582 20912 9

Henry VIII (Second edition)
M D Palmer   0 582 35437 4

Tudor Rebellions (Fourth edition)
Anthony Fletcher & Diarmaid MacCulloch   0 582 28990 4

The Reign of Mary I (Second edition)
Robert Tittler   0 582 06107 5

Early Tudor Parliaments 1485–1558
Michael A R Graves   0 582 03497 3

The English Reformation 1530–1570
W J Sheils   0 582 35398 X

Elizabethan Parliaments 1559–1601 (Second edition)
Michael A R Graves   0 582 29196 8

England and Europe 1485–1603 (Second edition)
Susan Doran   0 582 28991 2

The Church of England 1570–1640
Andrew Foster   0 582 35574 5

STUART BRITAIN

Social Change and Continuity: England 1550–1750 (Second edition)
Barry Coward   0 582 29442 8

James I (Second edition)
S J Houston   0 582 20911 0

The English Civil War 1640–1649
Martyn Bennett   0 582 35392 0

Charles I, 1625–1640
Brian Quintrell   0 582 00354 7

The English Republic 1649–1660 (Second edition)
Toby Barnard   0 582 08003 7

Radical Puritans in England 1550–1660
R J Acheson   0 582 35515 X

The Restoration and the England of Charles H (Second edition)
John Miller   0 582 29223 9

The Glorious Revolution (Second edition)
John Miller   0 582 29222 0

EARLY MODERN EUROPE

The Renaissance (Second edition)
Alison Brown   0 582 30781 3

The Emperor Charles V
Martyn Rady   0 582 35475 7

French Renaissance Monarchy: Francis I and Henry II (Second edition)
Robert Knecht   0 582 28707 3

The Protestant Reformation in Europe
Andrew Johnston   0 582 07020 1

The French Wars of Religion 1559–1598 (Second edition)
Robert Knecht   0 582 28533 X

Phillip II
Geoffrey Woodward   0 582 07232 8

The Thirty Years' War
Peter Limm   0 582 35373 4

Louis XIV
Peter Campbell   0 582 01770 X

Spain in the Seventeenth Century
Graham Darby   0 582 07234 4

Peter the Great
William Marshall   0 582 00355 5

EUROPE 1789–1918

Britain and the French Revolution
Clive Emsley   0 582 36961 4

Revolution and Terror in France 1789–1795 (Second edition)
D G Wright   0 582 00379 2

Napoleon and Europe
D G Wright   0 582 35457 9

Nineteenth-Century Russia: Opposition to Autocracy
Derek Offord   0 582 35767 5

The Constitutional Monarchy in France 1814–48
Pamela Pilbeam   0 582 31210 8

The 1848 Revolutions (Second edition)
Peter Jones   0 582 06106 7

The Italian Risorgimento
M Clark   0 582 00353 9

Bismark & Germany 1862–1890 (Second edition)
D G Williamson   0 582 29321 9

Imperial Germany 1890–1918
Ian Porter, Ian Armour and Roger Lockyer   0 582 03496 5

The Dissolution of the Austro-Hungarian Empire 1867–1918 (Second edition)
John W Mason   0 582 29466 5

Second Empire and Commune: France 1848–1871 (Second edition)
William H C Smith   0 582 28705 7

France 1870–1914 (Second edition)
Robert Gildea   0 582 29221 2

The Scramble for Africa (Second edition)
M E Chamberlain   0 582 36881 2

Late Imperial Russia 1890–1917
John F Hutchinson   0 582 32721 0

The First World War
Stuart Robson   0 582 31556 5

EUROPE SINCE 1918

The Russian Revolution (Second edition)
Anthony Wood   0 582 35559 1

Lenin's Revolution: Russia, 1917–1921
David Marples   0 582 31917 X

Stalin and Stalinism (Second edition)
Martin McCauley   0 582 27658 6

The Weimar Republic (Second edition)
John Hiden   0 582 28706 5

The Inter-War Crisis 1919–1939
Richard Overy   0 582 35379 3

Fascism and the Right in Europe, 1919–1945
Martin Blinkhorn   0 582 07021 X

Spain's Civil War (Second edition)
Harry Browne   0 582 28988 2

The Third Reich (Second edition)
D G Williamson   0 582 20914 5

The Origins of the Second World War (Second edition)
R J Overy   0 582 29085 6

The Second World War in Europe
Paul MacKenzie   0 582 32692 3

Anti-Semitism before the Holocaust
Albert S Lindemann   0 582 36964 9

The Holocaust: The Third Reich and the Jews
David Engel   0 582 32720 2

Germany from Defeat to Partition, 1945–1963
D G Williamson   0 582 29218 2

Britain and Europe since 1945
Alex May   0 582 30778 3

Eastern Europe 1945–1969: From Stalinism to Stagnation
Ben Fowkes   0 582 32693 1

The Khrushchev Era, 1953–1964
Martin McCauley   0 582 27776 0

NINETEENTH-CENTURY BRITAIN

Britain before the Reform Acts: Politics and Society 1815–1832
Eric J Evans   0 582 00265 6

Parliamentary Reform in Britain c. 1770–1918
Eric J Evans   0 582 29467 3

Democracy and Reform 1815–1885
D G Wright   0 582 31400 3

Poverty and Poor Law Reform in Nineteenth-Century Britain, 1834–1914:
From Chadwick to Booth
David Englander   0 582 31554 9

The Birth of Industrial Britain: Economic Change, 1750–1850
Kenneth Morgan   0 582 29833 4

Chartism (Third edition)
Edward Royle   0 582 29080 5

Peel and the Conservative Party 1830–1850
Paul Adelman   0 582 35557 5

Gladstone, Disraeli and later Victorian Politics (Third edition)
Paul Adelman   0 582 29322 7

Britain and Ireland: From Home Rule to Independence
Jeremy Smith   0 582 30193 9

TWENTIETH-CENTURY BRITAIN

The Rise of the Labour Party 1880–1945 (Third edition)
Paul Adelman   0 582 29210 7

The Conservative Party and British Politics 1902–1951
Stuart Ball   0 582 08002 9

The Decline of the Liberal Party 1910–1931 (Second edition)
Paul Adelman   0 582 27733 7

The British Women's Suffrage Campaign 1866–1928
Harold L Smith   0 582 29811 3

War & Society in Britain 1899–1948
Rex Pope   0 582 03531 7

The British Economy since 1914: A Study in Decline?
Rex Pope   0 582 30194 7

Unemployment in Britain between the Wars
Stephen Constantine   0 582 35232 0

The Attlee Governments 1945–1951
Kevin Jefferys   0 582 06105 9

The Conservative Governments 1951–1964
Andrew Boxer   0 582 20913 7

Britain under Thatcher
Anthony Seldon and Daniel Collings   0 582 31714 2

INTERNATIONAL HISTORY

The Eastern Question 1774–1923 (Second edition)
A L Macfie   0 582 29195 X

The Origins of the First World War (Second edition)
Gordon Martel   0 582 28697 2

The United States and the First World War
Jennifer D Keene   0 582 35620 2

Anti-Semitism before the Holocaust
Albert S Lindemann   0 582 36964 9

The Origins of the Cold War, 1941–1949 (Second edition)
Martin McCauley   0 582 27659 4

Russia, America and the Cold War, 1949–1991
Martin McCauley   0 582 27936 4

The Arab–Israeli Conflict
Kirsten E Schulze   0 582 31646 4

The United Nations since 1945: Peacekeeping and the Cold War
Norrie MacQueen   0 582 35673 3

Decolonisation: The British Experience since 1945
Nicholas J White   0 582 29087 2

The Vietnam War
Mitchell Hall   0 582 32859 4

WORLD HISTORY

China in Transformation, 1900–1949
Colin Mackerras   0 582 31209 4

Japan in Transformation, 1952–2000
Jeff Kingston   0 582 41875 5

US HISTORY

America in the Progressive Era, 1890–1914
Lewis L Gould   0 582 35671 7

The United States and the First World War
Jennifer D Keene   0 582 35620 2

The Truman Years, 1945–1953
Mark S Byrnes   0 582 32904 3

The Vietnam War
Mitchell Hall   0 582 32859 4

American Abolitionists
Stanley Harrold   0 582 35738 1

The American Civil War, 1861–1865
Reid Mitchell   0 582 31973 0